TURNS OUT:

21 years on

THE BIG SUR RIVER

BY BARBARA DELMAR

To Rick, who bought the place for me, to go on our grand adventure; and to Brian, who built the bridge, and made us laugh the whole time.

Table of Contents

Forward

People seem to want to know about Big Sur. My sister has traveled the world, and said she can start a conversation with anyone, anywhere, by telling them her sister lives in Big Sur. So many people want to visit, so many more people than the infrastructure was built to handle, it's becoming difficult for both visitors and locals alike. That makes writing about Big Sur complicated. I want to share my story. I don't want my story to have a negative impact on my dear neighbors, who were so kind to me.

We were so private while living there, very few locals knew we existed, let alone our names, or where we lived. Everyone who lives in Big Sur values their privacy, too; that's why they live there. With that in mind, I have distorted my descriptions of our area, and changed some names. I've used a pen name, too. But the stories are all true, to the best of my recollection.

Part 1: Turns Out

It's an Unusual Property

"It's an unusual property," the real estate agent said. "Oh? How so?" I asked. "There's an access issue. Sometimes, in the winter rainy season, you'll have to use a swinging footbridge to get to the house, but only when the river is too high to cross in a 4x4." Wow! We'll have to cross the river to get to the house? What's a swinging footbridge, I wondered. We were so naive, we didn't understand "unusual" was a legal real estate term.

I thought about the bridge in the Indiana Jones movie, you know, made of rope, suspended across a deep chasm, with round branches laid down as floorboards to walk across. I said, "That *is* unusual." I asked if we would be able to pull a wagon across the bridge, like a kid's wagon filled with groceries, and she said "Oh yes, you could!" Okay then. I made plans to see the property that weekend. I asked how often we'd have to use the bridge, and she said, "Oh, not very often at all." Turns out, we used that bridge every day.

We had no intention of buying the place when I made the appointment, we were planning on wasting the poor real estate agent's time, when you come right down to it. And we didn't understand then that we would be wasting a really significant amount of her time, since the property was so far away from everything.

The picture we saw in the brochure was so small, it's hard to believe it could make such a big difference in our lives, but I knew as soon as we saw it, I wanted to be there. There were gigantic, elegant redwoods surrounding a lovely redwood home, and the front wall of the house was 2 stories of windows, with a beautiful redwood deck. Just thinking about it still makes my heart race. The caption said there was a river behind the house, too. Well, that really piqued my interest. I had just become aware of a beautiful little bird, the black phoebe, who lives by water sources like creeks and rivers. I'm a bird lover, and I really wanted to see that bird, so much so that I had begun to create a fake creek in our back yard to attract it.

2   It's an Unusual Property

We were newly married, middle-aged folks with no children, and my husband worked mostly from home, which meant living in Big Sur was possible. We wanted to play the part of interested shoppers, to get to see the house, river, bird, and now swinging bridge! Imagine that, a house you couldn't get to without crossing a footbridge! What a fun day trip this would be, and I would finally get to see Big Sur, the mysterious, ultra-hip, beautiful and beloved Big Sur! We had no idea what we were in for.

"It's an unusual property," she said again when we met her. We just thought she was making a pithy comment. Later, after touring the property, we thought it was an understatement, and being lovers of nature and the unusual, we decided to buy it. Considering our intentions, it was a case of instant karma, or, two acres of instant karma, if you prefer.

That weekend, when we went to see the house, it was a very hot and sunny day in Mountain View, but it was cool and shady there in the forest. The canopy was completely closed and the largest spot of sun I saw was not large enough to warm two people. But the Redwoods were fabulous! They were the largest group of large diameter Redwoods I had ever seen, outside of Big Basin park. I could hardly believe anyone was allowed to own such a treasure.

The property had more than 30 redwoods that are larger than two feet in diameter, even though it's only two acres. That includes two 1000 year old trees, three 800 year old trees, and on the park adjacent there are many other giant, seriously old growth trees, too. But I'm a bit ahead of myself.

We turned off the highway and drove through grassy meadows, along a nearly half mile winding driveway. We parked up there behind the massive gate (and mail box), which was open for us, and we walked, or rather, slipped down the rest of the driveway, it was so steep. We entered a shade that was dark and instantaneous, and we passed all kinds of plant life just reaching out to touch us the whole way. There were so many shades of green, we couldn't see where the driveway ended, it just disappeared in the green. But after a bit, we could see a woman waving to us, and we introduced ourselves and started to seriously look around, and I think this is where our chins first dropped.

It was beautiful, green and quiet, the air was clean, moist and easy to breath in. I think we spent the whole showing looking up with our mouths open, saying "Wow!" You just don't see a 1500 year old redwood tree that is 10 feet in diameter every day. It's a once-in-a-lifetime thing, and there it was, on what could just possibly be our property. OUR property!

Since Terry didn't have a 4-wheel drive, and we didn't either, we had to walk across the "swinging footbridge," which really should have been called the "bouncing footbridge." The walking surface of the bridge was not level, and it tilted from side to side with every step we took. With three of us walking, it was like an amusement park ride. We had to hold onto the side railings to keep from being thrown off the bridge, and those railings were not at an even height the entire way across. They were very low in the middle, so even though I'm short, I had to bend down to reach them. That made it even more likely to be thrown off the middle of the bridge, right over the water and rocks.

Scary as that was, it was so stunningly beautiful, we couldn't speak. As we crossed the bridge we could see up and down stream and the view was enough to stop us in our tracks. There were trees so dense on both sides of the river that we couldn't see what was beyond the banks, we could only see the tree tops as they rose to the top of the ridge to the west. Many of the trees that lined the river's edge were reaching out to each other, as if their branches were trying to hold hands, and some of them succeeded, so the river water was shaded and cold as it tumbled over the rocky bottom.

The sound of the river tumbling and tinkling by could have been the music of the Big Sur Pied Piper, calling me home. The whole environment was new and yet familiar, exciting and calming, it was the future of my life beckoning me with both arms, saying, "This is the way..." We hadn't even seen the house yet, and I already felt such a strong connection to this place, it overwhelmed me. I was taking the biggest breath of my life.

Most delightfully of all, there was enough water in the river to tumble by us. California had been enduring one of it's longest droughts at that time, seven years of conserving water, seven years of news about how little water we had, yet there was water in this river, with fish swimming and birds flitting through the biggest trees I'd ever seen. When we told Jerry, who rented the small cabin on the property, we were surprised to see the water, he said, almost indignantly, "We get 40 inches of rain a year, of course there's water in the river." So this was water country, there was no drought here. We stepped into a magical garden when we made that turn off the highway.

The swinging footbridge, now that was an unreal reality. As we slipped down the driveway, we slipped beneath some taut wires that were one end of the suspension wires holding up the bridge. Terry said the wires were anchored in that hill above the driveway by a six foot by six foot by six foot concrete block that she called a "deadman." The bridge was about 175 feet long and the walkway was three 10 inch wide boards, side by side, making about a 32 inch wide walkway.

Most of the wood was old and painted a gray color that makes things appear even older than they are. The wires were very old, rusty and thin in some places; a year later, one broke as a guest was crossing it. The whole bridge looked to be in such bad shape, I'm not sure I would have walked across if I hadn't been following Terry and distracted by the beauty of the river scene. Plus, the bridge was higher on one side of the river than the other, and it sagged a bit in the middle, so no matter which direction we were going, we had to go uphill at the end.

Oh, but it was glorious! Standing there in the middle, we could see the trees that grew along the sides of the river were different than the ones we passed on the way down the driveway, they were almost lacy with tall, grayish white trunks and dark green, oval leaves with serrated edges. We could see this because the bridge was 20 some feet off the ground, and we were up there, among the branches.

These were delicate branches with the most delicate of birds twittering and flitting from branch to branch. The birds were chickadees and warblers, hunting on what I found out later were red alder trees. The sun beaming down on the river in small spots made the water look like sparkling gems. The tiny birds singing against the background of the river's tinkling were the only sounds to pierce the utter quiet we stepped into. Against the green of the giant redwoods that formed the background to everything there, this seemed a magical experience come to life. It seemed I could raise my hand and a little chickadee would land on it. I was so taken by the scene, a bird could have pooped on my head and I still would have wanted to be there.

I could have stayed there in the middle of the bridge for hours, but Terry had a job to do and we had to play along. So we followed her to the end of the bridge where the real forest began. We walked into a wood so dense and dark, the shade of the forest was like a character in it's own right; strong, cool, dominate shade, even though it was a really bright, hot day. I melt in the sun and heat, and feeling how cool it was in the shade under the redwoods was so comfortable, so right.

The path from the bridge to the house wound past giant redwood trees and what we came to find out were 100 foot tall Tanoaks with 2½ foot diameter trunks. There were various large sizes of Coast Live Oak, Big Leaf Maple, California Laurel, and Sycamore. It was so dense, we could only see about 10 feet or so into the woods off the path, and we really didn't want to get lost, so we kept up with Terry.

To the sides of the path were beautiful ferns, and flowers I had never seen before, with lots of giant clover. There were small plants that had little bell shaped flowers hiding, dangling, under the green leaves. They were called Fairy Bells, because only the tiny fairies could see them, but I could see them because they were growing on one of the many giant logs laying about, from old growth trees that had fallen and hadn't been removed. Some sections had been cut out of them to clear paths for walking and driving, and every one of those logs was covered in a thick layer of emerald green moss, and did I mention ferns?

We passed a shed and the small cabin that Jerry lived in, and then went past some more giant redwoods, 5 to 8 feet in diameter. These trees are majestic. They're 500 to 1000 years old and there's a whole world of living spaces on each branch. Each group of redwoods is like it's own country, with lots of residents, visitors and wild animal folks, hoping not to be discovered.

Then we saw the house. Calling it our "California Dream House" is both an understatement and an overstatement. It was a total fixer-upper, and we had no idea how to fixer-up. On the other hand, if we had known anything about construction, we'd have walked, no, run, far, far away, and missed out on the adventure. But reality was not required of us on this particular day-trip, so we left it home.

As we toured the house, Terry told us the history of the property; the house had been built in 1968, during the height of hippie life, by a man who was a young, high-priced hippie lawyer, and he intended it to be his summer party house. We heard about people driving Cadillacs across the river to come to parties there, and we heard that some of the parties were political. We heard some of these stories after we had been living there for years, from tourists from other countries who stopped by to see if it was still a "party house."

Apparently, the young lawyer had big parties that included his clients, and Supreme Court Chief Justice Earl Warren had been at one of his parties, and Angela Davis at another. We also heard that this lawyer's father had been a member of California state government in the late 30's, and that he had bought the property to be his summer home. She told us that before he moved in there, he had the phone lines extended from Point Sur, where they ended, south to the valley, to this property, so he could be in touch with other government officials even though he was spending his summers in the woods with his family. And of course, he, too, had big parties with many dignitaries, one of which was Supreme Court Chief Justice Warren Berger. So both ends of the political spectrum had attended parties on this property, and that added to the historical cachet.

Terry told us it was the same engineers and workers that brought the phone lines down the coast who built the suspension bridge, using the same parts they used to get the phones there, plus some wood floorboards. They built the bridge in 1950. Shortly after, the old Restaurant and Dance Hall they had been using as their summer home was crushed by a falling redwood, and that's when they built the little cabin Jerry was living in, that we passed by on the path to the house. They used redwood they milled from trees that already lay on the ground around them.

Turns out the tag "unusual" applied to the house, not just the property, as the house was one room with a loft bedroom above, and a sunken section, too. Split level homes were the height of fashion in 1968 and everything that could have a split level in this house was split. The stairway had 3 levels and 3 turns to get to the bathroom and bedroom loft. But the beauty of the house came from the view outside because the house had 32 windows, and most were large, like 55" x 58". There were sliding glass doors that were nine feet wide, with giant windows above so we could see to the tops of the redwoods. Those doors and windows were on both the front and back of the house, so we could watch the river out the back windows and turn our head to see the forest out the front windows. It was like being outside, but bug free.

The house was built from old growth trees. Beautiful, fine grained Redwood and Douglas fir that had been cut down and milled in the 1890's in Santa Cruz, when all the trees there were old growth. The wood was first used to build a lumber yard warehouse in Santa Cruz that was in business selling lumber from 1900 until the 1960's, when the business and building was dismantled and the young lawyer moved the used lumber to Big Sur to build his new house. This wood had never been sanded and the roughness of it caused an abundance of inches-long splinters over the years. There were odd cut outs in the wood where it had been fit together with something in the past, leaving evidence to ponder.

The house was considered to be over-engineered, with giant 6x8 Redwood beams holding up huge roof boards that were 2½ inches thick by nearly 13 inches wide and up to 30 feet long. There are still some very old nails in that house that can't be pulled out of the wood, nails that were flat, not round. When I tried to date them, searching on-line I found estimates that they were made in the mid to late 1800's, which fits with what we were told about the lumber.

These nails look hand made, and they don't have flat heads. The nails are like a "T" that was punched out of a thick metal sheet and the tip sharpened. Showing the nails to our guests and talking about how the nails were made and who might have pounded them into those beams over a hundred years ago, that was one of the great topics of conversation we had in the house. Talk about unique.

8   It's an Unusual Property

The young lawyer wanted to have a house that he felt safe in, one that wouldn't be crushed by a falling redwood like the restaurant had been, so he hired an architect from Palo Alto to design such a building, using the lumber he had. The house was reinforced at the peak, the pitch to the roof was very steep, and it looked like any tree that hit the building straight on would break at that peak and NOT crush the building.

Years later, when we wanted to sell the house, we had two different architects evaluate that claim, both were from Big Sur and had experience with building around redwoods, and both found the claim credible under the building circumstances. But a tree that fell from the side of the house would tilt the house, flatten it and crush anyone inside. But a 50% reduction in risk is nothing to sneeze at!

The house had some really delightful aspects, too. It had clerestory windows that we could see redwood tree tops through, while we were lying in bed. For almost five years we could see what looked like a topiary of Rocky and Bullwinkle talking to each other, but it was actually the top branches of a redwood tree. We didn't even have to lift our heads off the pillows to see that. We had a door off our bedroom that opened to a little deck, that led to the hillside, where we could look up at the big, fat, leaning, moss covered tree trunks.

In the kitchen and bathroom, the counter tops were made of thick redwood slabs that were clearly old growth, with a dark marine varnish. They were dinged up and not flat, but they were still beautiful and useful. The grain of this wood is so very tight, it looks like the lines were drawn on with the finest point technical pen, and as closely together as possible with a barely perceptible space between the lines.

The windows were placed with a nod to the view, very tall windows in the stairwell showed the very wide trunks of the seven foot diameter redwood that was just eight inches away; skylights in the kitchen and bath allowed us to watch the pine cones fall straight down as if they would hit us in the face. Not one of the 32 windows was a standard size, and no two were alike. One was a triangle and one next to that was 55 inches wide with an angle on the top that matched the angle of the steep roof.

But the house hadn't been lived in for a while, and was clearly in need of work. There was so much to do, and I don't know why I thought it would be so simple to do it all, it really wasn't, but that Big Sur Pied Piper knew my tune, and played it over and over again. Such a delightful tune!

After touring the house, we walked out "back," which was really to the *side* of the house, but at the back of the property. We came to call that area the *Back Point Forty*, since large land owners are known to use the term Back Forty to refer to the remote area of their land. Ours was not so big or remote. But it turns out the layout of the land was one of the most irritating things about living there, the front door and windows on the front of the house did not face the path or the driveway. There were just two windows facing that direction, so we couldn't easily see who was coming to our door. Having to make five turns to get into the bathroom in the middle of the night was pretty irritating, and getting splinters just walking from the living room to the kitchen, past those rough cut 6x8 beams, was pretty irritating, too. But we saw no negatives that day.

Out back there was a whole acre with so many trees we could barely see the spur of the hill that led to the only ridge between us and the ocean. The ocean was about two miles as the crow flies, but you couldn't exactly get to the ocean that way without climbing up the ridge and falling off the cliff on the ocean side. We never tried that, but we did hear from folks who live up there that sometimes they see crazy tourists who have climbed the hill and pushed through the bushes on the edge of their property, to ask where the beach is.

We did climb the spur to see where the property line was and when we got up there we were dumbfounded all over again. Looking down on the property from up there was disorienting at first, the trees are so tall, there's kind of a weird disconnect. Maybe it's because while you are using switchbacks to climb the hill, you pass the same redwoods that are growing on the valley floor next to the house, pass them more than once, but their trunks seem almost the same size diameter at the top of the hill as at the bottom.

Looking down, things looks surreal and tiny, especially next to the huge redwoods. As we climbed higher, the air got more dry, and warm, and even though we were still in the shade, there was a lot more light, the shade wasn't as dense and didn't seem as important a part of the picture up there. When we got just over the property line, in what was called "green space" on the maps, we could see the big, blue, blue ocean, with a huge blue sky to match.

The trees and plants up there were different, too, and there weren't as many ferns, but there were more broad leaf trees and clumps of grass that had tiny white flower bracts that were fluffy, lacy and beautiful over the deep green of the tall blades. I miss seeing that grass, it was truly unusual. And even up there it was quiet. But we could understand from that hike that the redwood trees have different environments at different heights, and even the needles of redwood trees change shape from the bottom branches to the top branches.

Terry showed us the lay of the land from up there - the property was almost the shape of a triangle with one end cut off, and the longest side was down the middle of the river. The smaller sides were bordered by green space, and we had a couple of neighbors, three to eight acres away, on the other side of the green space.

Turns out we weren't just naive, we weren't good fake-buyers, either. Everything we said to Terry about the property was true. We loved it and we couldn't hide it, even though our plan was to tour the place and say it didn't meet our expectations. We made every buy sign known to man; we talked about how to keep tourists out, which we thought would be a big problem. (Tourists were a lot less trouble to locals during the years we lived there than they are today.) We talked about wanting to rebuild the bridge, about building a second bedroom, about where to put our desks. We asked almost no real questions about the house, and we neglected to ask the most important question - how much does it cost to remove a redwood? - because it never occurred to us that we might have to do that. We were tree-huggers and wanted to save every tree. Every one.

Usually, I try to imagine the worst that could happen in every situation, that way, I am happily surprised by life, not repeatedly disappointed. But this place was like a fairy tale, and I just could not imagine anything terrible happening there, besides flood. We had been told that there was a flood in 1983 in which the river rose more than 25 feet, and there was a foot of water covering the property, but the water didn't enter the houses.

The flood happened when the river was blocked downstream by a mudslide near the River Inn, which finally broke through because of the amount of water backed up behind it. Our bridge was floating at that point and when the dam broke, the water rushed downstream so quickly, it took the bridge with it. When it disconnected from the deadman on one side of the river, it floated to the other side, where it was reclaimed when the water receded, and was reattached with some additional wood and wire where needed. Sounds okay, right?

We really should have asked more questions about exactly how that side had been "reattached." Turns out, it hadn't been reattached to the "deadman" at all. The deadman was still there, of course, just not at the end of those wires. When we repaired the bridge six years later, we found the suspension wires had been attached to giant augers drilled in the ground, like the ones they use to keep telephone poles standing straight. That same size. Just two. We had had a 425 lb. pellet stove wheeled across that bridge by two very large gentlemen, and later, a crew of workers delivered 32 new double pane windows, every one carried across the bridge. We couldn't believe it was still hanging.

So two augers held up the east end of the bridge, and the west end of the bridge was held up by wrapping the wires around a 1000 year old redwood. Such good use of resources! And it turns out almost no bank will loan mortgage money for a property with a structure attached to a natural resource like a tree. Live and learn. Oh, the learning!

I felt a need to check out the health of the redwoods before we actually bought the property because I thought it would be agony to buy a piece of property largely because it had certain trees, only to see them die off after we moved in. I spent some time looking closely at the trees, and found some holes in the bark of the big trees that I wondered about. They were about the size of a quarter, and they had different depths, but they all went straight in. I looked in books at bookstores and in my own garden books, but I found nothing.

There was no real Internet yet, so I couldn't do my "own" research, I had to actually ask people. I asked at garden centers and called a few Universities. I don't know how many, but probably enough to be a pain in the butt to a number of people. I asked professors of entomology if they knew of any bugs that would make holes like that in the bark of the redwoods, or was there any fungus or other thing that would do this to redwoods, that would cause trouble for the trees. No one knew of any bugs or any other reason there would be such holes in the bark of the trees.

Apparently, bugs don't like redwoods. I didn't see any bug poop, excuse me, excrement, around any of the holes, I didn't see any sawdust either, so no one had any answers for me. The real estate agent said the trees were healthy, and they looked healthy, so I decided to believe they were healthy. I didn't know I could call an Arborist. I don't know how long it took me, months or years, but I do remember being totally embarrassed when I finally realized the holes were left by branches from when the trees were younger, that have since fallen off. I'm turning red just thinking about it.

But I missed an opportunity to learn what I should have been interested in learning, and that is, how much does it cost to remove a tree? A BIG tree? Well, we found it cost - $10,000 in 2007 to remove a redwood tree that was 200 feet tall and seven feet diameter, which I'll talk more about later. But when I look back now, I can't imagine why we didn't try to find out those costs before we bought. It turns out, naivety is the most costly thing of all.

Hurricane Andrew was soon to hit Florida, and a few years later I read an article in a garden magazine by a survivor, about how all their trees had been broken and killed by the hurricane. The author had to remove the 60 trees on their acre of land and wrote about how hard that was, emotionally and financially. Neither one of us had owned a tree before. We didn't understand the responsibility involved, only the beauty, the shade, the romance. And at the time, no one knew that Sudden Oak Death was about to take off and kill millions of oak, tanoak and laurel trees across the west coast, and that it was already at, and would decimate our property.

So, with our heads in the trees, we fell totally in love with the place. We checked with Rick's office, and got their okay to move so far away, work from home and only come into the office two days a week. Then we worked on the financing and made our offer. Turns out, to add insult to injury, we overpaid. We could probably have gotten it for a lot less, but we didn't know they were in foreclosure, and we were so inexperienced with real estate, we didn't even know that was something we could have found out. There was no Internet Real Estate business at that time, everything was still on paper and local, we'd have had to go to the county to find that out. But it was just supposed to be a day trip, just a fun day in Big Sur. We weren't supposed to have to know any of these things.

Before we made our final decision, we checked all around the Bay Area and found no comparable houses that had the unique pleasures of this house. It was on a wooded and cool lot, had unlimited water supplies, and was within five miles of a store where we could buy milk, which was a really big deal to me. There was a full service garage, also very important to me, a fine restaurant, and a fire department, all nearby the milk store. And the doctors office was close by, too. This was better than anything we could find in the suburbs of the Bay Area. There was even an engineering company who could help us with the bridge. We thought all these things were important.

Turns out we only went to the restaurant a few times in 20 years and we never bought milk at that store. But the Health Center was so caring, you'd have thought they were concierge doctors, but no, they just actually cared, and I miss them all. Blaze Engineering had everything we ever needed to keep things running properly, and saved our butts on numerous occasions, at times within 15 minutes of our call. And I had become so dependent on the garage, I cried when it closed. It wasn't just that cars are so important to life in Big Sur. It's that I wouldn't have moved there if the garage hadn't been there, I couldn't imagine living in such a remote place with out an expert mechanic to call on. It really was a security blanket for me. And Jali, the owner, was too kind to ever make us feel foolish, even when we had been. He came to our rescue so many times, and I'll always be grateful.

We met with the owner of the house before we made an offer, and he took us to dinner in the fine restaurant. He asked us if we wanted to stay in the house the next weekend. We were thrilled. He told us personal stories about time spent there while he was growing up. He told us about the time when, under orders from his father, he disassembled a wine vat in Santa Cruz and reassembled it on the hill to be the water tank. He told us about driving his Cadillac over the river. He told us about the three different trucks that had been flattened when branches from Old Tom fell on them.

His dad was kind of a tyrant who disliked lawyers and artists, so one son became a lawyer and the other an artist. We were buying it from the artist, who had bought it from the lawyer, who inherited it from the father. He told us he was the first to walk across the bridge when it was built, after his father said, "Go ahead, Tom, you're expendable, you go first." The sons found great pleasure in choosing their careers. It was a delightful evening.

That weekend was July 4th. We had some idea that we could handle roughing it, and we were excited. As we headed down Highway One, it was foggy in Monterey, and by the time we got to Carmel, it was drizzling. We found it rains there almost every July 4th weekend, or sometime during that week. It's not a rainstorm, just a drizzle, but we came to love and look forward to that drizzle, it's so refreshing. At the time we thought another couple was touring the house in the morning, and we hoped the rain would put them off. Looking back with more knowledge about real estate transactions, I don't think there was ever another couple at all.

But we loved the place, we thought we paid a reasonably fair price, considering how much higher prices were in the Bay Area at the time, and the lifestyle Big Sur would afford us. Living in a wooded setting is valuable and the homes we found in the Bay Area in the same price range were in bad neighborhoods and had no redwoods. We'd have had to spend another $200k to get redwoods, and even these houses were far from a milk store, on very steep slopes, no river, no auto repair garage, too warm and had too many people, visible people, nearby.

From the house in Big Sur we couldn't see other houses, cars, signs, businesses, lights, or even the highway, even though that was all relatively close. We couldn't even see our own cars parked on the other side of the river. More important and even more unique in Big Sur, no other neighbors had to use our driveway or fire road to get to their house. True solitude. Absolute quiet. We wanted to live alone in the woods and this was the only place we saw where that was truly possible.

I once heard my husband say, "With a house in the suburbs, there aren't too many negatives, and there aren't excessive positives, either. Living in Big Sur, the positives are astronomical, so it doesn't matter that the costs and negatives are nearly so, too." Neither one of us really understood before we moved there how anyone could fall in love with a property, with a place. But we know now.

Of course, living in the country can take a financial toll at the same time it's providing emotional wellbeing. It's costs a lot to live rurally, even if you're hermits like we were. When we moved in, Rick said he thought it would cost everything we already had, and half of everything we would ever have. But it turns out that everything we will ever have is only half of what we needed to stay. We don't go out to dinner, or buy alcohol by the glass at bars, but there are costs we didn't know enough to take into consideration.

It's just more expensive to live in the country, and the further out you go, the more it costs to get supplies. What you're really paying for is a peaceful environment where you can interact with the natural world, where you can breath deeply without bothering anyone else. Without being bothered by the sights, sounds and smells of other people. When our friend John came from San Jose to visit, he said, "Wow! You can talk as loud as you want out here. You never have to be quiet!" That freedom, that space is valuable to my psyche, and as our population gets larger and larger, it becomes more and more valuable, personally as well as financially. We'd have paid a million for that place if we'd had it.

And looking back, I can see that those years in Big Sur were the best years of our lives. Other people I've met who have moved away are trying to get back to Big Sur, to recreate the happiness they felt there. The happiness is addicting, I wish everyone could feel it. The peacefulness, the beauty, the danger is addicting. And the strength you gain mentally and physically from the hard work required to survive in such a beautiful, yet extremely difficult environment is very satisfying.

Like that time the river was raging, it was dark, the wind was howling, rain was pouring down and an alder tree was being pressed up against the bridge by the flow of the river. The bridge was so rickety, we could see the alder would take the whole bridge down. We had only been there a few months and didn't have a chainsaw. Why would we need a chain saw? We didn't want to cut trees down, we wanted to protect them. I think that, right there, is the most idiotic thought I've ever had. A real lack of understanding.

So we only had a curved hand saw with big teeth that was meant to cut four inch branches, and this tree was more like 10 inches in diameter. But you work with what you have in an emergency. We went out on the bridge and Rick started to cut the tree, which was slow-going and hard work because of all the bouncing and the trunk banging on the bridge. A smooth cut was not possible in that case. We didn't know exactly which direction to try to make the tree fall. We didn't want it to fall on the bridge, but he couldn't reach high enough to cut so the top would fall over the bridge and into the downstream water.

The only place he could really cut was at the height of the railing. He started cutting there, and he saved the bridge. The tree fell into the water just fine. But he *was* nearly killed by the tree. The water was moving so fast, the tree didn't have time to sink in, and I watched as it came right back up to Rick, cut end first, and it just about pushed him over the other railing and into the water, he barely had time to get out of the way. Not a survivable fall and a very close call.

The river was so high, and just four feet below us, so loud, and moving so fast that anything in it becomes a projectile of sorts. But the tree top did finally make it under the bridge, and only some branches got caught up in the bridge, but not enough to be a problem. So Rick saved our bridge and his life that day and that's the kind of event that can make you sloppy happy with life. I'm not saying that we moved to the woods to have experiences like this, but passing tests like this, exerting some control over your world, can be very satisfying, if you survive.

After living there a few years, I told my sister that I dreamed of having a place up the hill where we could have a concrete pad with a small shed that had supplies for living during a flood emergency, and she said, "Dream? That sounds like a nightmare to me!" We never got that shed together, but we did spend two months there in '98 without being able to leave town at all because of bad roads, and we were evacuated for fire once, too. Good times... Even after that, we still loved the place, and wanted to stay forever. Every hardship you survive makes you just a little bit more confident that you can survive the next one. Survive a few, and you're on your way to being called "stoic." It was a new way of getting to know ourselves.

Before we moved in, we made a list of all the things we thought we would need to live happily there. On the top of the list was a generator and battery back-up system for our computers. It was the smartest thing we did. I had read about people being stuck in Big Sur for over a year because of mudslides, and if that happened to us, Rick would still need to work using his computer, so we would still need power and phone to network with the office.

We bought gas cans to store gas, and we planned to have a week of gas on hand at all times. We would need to run the generator to pump water into the water tank, too, because a full tank really only lasted 2 days. We added flashlights, camp stove, propane and all the camping/emergency gear we could find to the list. And lots of water purification tablets, which I finally threw out years later, as we packed to move out. We used everything else, though. And we lusted after large trucks with big wheels, large wood chippers and bulldozers.

First River Crossing

We were supposed to meet the movers on Thursday morning at 7am, right where the driveway meets the highway, to start the process of having everything taken out of the moving van, loaded into a 4x4 pick-up truck, driven across the river and then unloaded at our house. It's not as uncommon as we thought, but it cost a lot of money. The movers didn't feel comfortable taking our electronics across the river, so we had to do that ourselves. We thought about taking them across the bridge, but we didn't think we could get them to the house without either losing them over the railing into the river, or bouncing them to death on the bridge. Safely tucked into a vehicle, padded and tied down seemed the way to go.

But U-haul didn't have the 4-wheel-drive vehicle to rent they said they would, so they gave us the highest riding van they had with the biggest tires, and we just had to hope all the stories about driving Cadillacs across had been true. We loaded up the van after all the movers had left the house at 8pm, then picked up some fast food, drove 3½ hours to the house and ate along the way. It was 1:30am and totally dark when we got there, I mean dark, no lights anywhere, no street lights, no business lights, no neighbors, and the moon was only a sliver in the sky, just three days before a new moon and barely helpful.

Neither of us had ever driven across a river before and frankly, we were true Babes in the Woods that night. We had been given no advice or instructions about this river-crossing endeavor, and we didn't even know we should be asking. It seemed like a creek to us anyway, not really a big deal, and with the drought, and it being so late in the year, we thought it was probably nearly empty anyway, so we plowed right through, just like we heard the owners used to do. Finally, our adventure was beginning! A very bouncy beginning, with much deeper water than we knew.

We got stuck just on the other side of the river, with one tire on dry land and three tires still underwater. We were so close, so very close. No matter how many times we tried to rock our way out of that spot, we couldn't. We were tired, so tired, and now scared, too, not just that we had damaged the van, but that we were doing something terrible to the environment and some local would come along any minute and castigate us for being idiots. It's amazing how quickly the woods can expose your inner idiocy. We were at an angle, with the back end of the van deeper in the water and the exhaust pipe under water. It took some discussion before we felt okay to turn off the engine. Then we had to climb out of the van and into the river, in the dark, without boots.

Did I mention that I can't swim and have a deathly fear of water? Just opening the van door to look out had been difficult, and now I had to put my feet and legs into that dark, very cold water, and it was deep of course, that's why we were stuck. I think this was probably the first time I thought to myself, "What are we doing here?" We had gone to so much trouble to get here, though, I didn't have the nerve to say that out loud to Rick. It was just a few months later, during a 100 mile per hour wind storm that we both said it out loud, nearly simultaneously, and then burst into laughter.

That night, I got wet up to the tops of my thighs, and part of the problem was the rocks were so slippery. Keeping my body upright as we climbed out was difficult, and I was really, really glad I didn't fall into that water. Rick seemed much more sanguine about the whole situation, and I didn't want to look like a pansy to my super cool, new husband, so I had to keep calm and carry on. And carry my little dog, Buddy, too.

We walked to the house in the barest of light, collecting sand and leaves to our wet pants and shoes as we walked. We had no flashlights with us because they had been packed in the moving van, and we couldn't see a single lit bulb anywhere. We almost felt our way to the house, trying to keep an eye out for mountain lions and coyotes while we searched for signs we actually were on the path, it was so dense with leaves and trees all around us.

We found our way to the house, the empty, empty house that had no food, bedding, TP, chairs or any other thing that could have made us comfortable. But we had one thing going for us, I had been there earlier that week to have the phones (land lines) installed, so we were able to call AAA.

Yes, AAA. And they came! It took more than an hour, but that lovely man was there with a beautiful, bright yellow tow truck at 3am to save us, and he was none too happy about it. He came from Carmel, and had been fast asleep when we called. But he backed the truck all the way down the long driveway to the edge of the water, which was pretty impressive right there, and he got a big, very bright light out and aimed it at the back of the van. It lit up an area about 20 feet diameter: I immediately wanted one, too, it was like daylight. He took a big, thick metal hook with a thick cable attached to it, off the back of the truck and held it up in the air in the light from the truck.

This was all great, except for one thing, he was still on the other side of the river. We had gotten back in the truck to await his arrival, so I opened the van door, leaned out and and called across the river to ask him what he was going to do with that hook. He yelled back, "I'm not getting wet. You'll have to come get this hook, take it back across the river and attach it to the rear axle of the van. Then I'll pull the van back across the river to this side." I started to panic and yelled back that we needed the van to be on this side of the river and he yelled, "*I'm not getting wet* or putting my truck in the river. Take it or leave it." Well, crap.

Rick was getting ready to make the trek across, but I had a sudden flash of clarity. I thought it was probably just the right time to conquer my fear of water and prove to myself that I really could handle it there. So I said to Rick, "I'll do it." He didn't want me to, but I told him I needed to do it. It was a long, slow walk, but there was enough light from the tow truck to see the individual rocks in the water, see they were covered with algae, so I was able to keep my balance, and more importantly, I could see clearly enough to know there were no giant sharks in the water to bite me. I could even see that there were no wild animals waiting to eat me or even just surprise me into slipping.

I brought the hook back, and Rick was in the water already to attach the hook to the van, and then we took a very fast and bumpy ride backwards across the river, strapped into the van with Buddy on my lap. The tow truck driver towed us to the highway and we left the van parked on the side of the road. The driver told us he would not come back that night, or tomorrow, to tow that van again, that the driveway was too steep for anything but a 4-wheel drive, we should not expect it to make it up the driveway even when the van was full, but especially not after we unloaded it and there was no weight in the back. He took off so fast, we couldn't even beg him to wait. I guess he had been called out by enough tourist idiots to know how to get the job done and get out of there. I don't blame him. I'm grateful he showed up.

It was a less than glorious introduction to our California Dream. Have you heard the phrase, "Experience is what you get when you don't get what you want?" This was the first of many experiences we had in our beloved Big Sur, where every property provides it's own unique experience; ours was the combination of river, trees, and steep valley, where others have steep ridge top, sky and ocean.

We had an air mattress and bedding in the van, though, and an overnight bag, and we had to carry that heavy load all the way down the driveway, across the bridge, and all the way to the house. We had to keep an eye on my little dog Buddy, too. I'm glad we were able to start this adventure in our early 40's, and didn't wait until we were retired and tired.

Even with the difficulties, it was still Paradise, and I had just proved to myself I had a larger reserve of inner strength than I knew, so I was ready to take on all the next challenges, starting with getting a good nights sleep in just three hours. We all trekked to the house for the second time that night, but by now we were adjusted to the light level and could see all the "spooky space," as we came to call it. And fear can really wake you up. Which was a good thing because we still had to set up the air mattress and put the bedding on it before we had a place to sleep, but I think I slept more soundly in the next three hours than I ever slept in my life.

The Repairs

Everything on the property needed repair or replacing. Everything. When we called contractors for estimates, we were warned that if we applied for county permits to replace anything, we would have to apply to the Coastal Commission for permits as well, which would cost a lot of money. My limited understanding of the situation is this: the Commission charges exorbitant fees for permits from anyone living near the coast, so they can use that money to buy ocean-front property for the public's use. Intellectually, we support that mission. We just couldn't support it financially. The agent who sold us the property did not inform us of this. She not only flat-out lied to us, but she left out so much info that was really important. So we really didn't understand that only wealthy people should buy property off Highway One. And once we were there, we were trapped, in paradise, where the worst thing that could happen was we would have to leave.

All we could do was repair what was there, to code, with pictures. And there were an enormous amount of repairs just because of the moisture in the environment from the rain every year, let alone the moisture in the air from the river. Where the suburbs of the Bay Area generally get 15 inches of rain, Big Sur's average is 40 inches. That's five feet of rain.

But we also heard horror stories about dealing with the planning department of the county. We heard they were understaffed and it took months just to get something as simple as a new hot water heater. We heard about one homeowner who was trying to repair one railing board on their own deck, and because a neighbor saw that, and reported that, the homeowner ended up spending $30,000 for the repair, counting permits from everybody under the sun and inspections finding more damage than the homeowner really wanted to repair at that time. We don't know how true any of that was, but we really didn't intend to break any laws. We were minimalists in that we didn't want to expand our holdings, we just wanted to keep them whole.

Generator & Battery Back-up

One of the first things we did was set up the generator and batteries. Like everything else, our generator setup was unusual. But we couldn't have lived there without it and we only had to replace the generator once. Both Briggs and Stratton engines, and wow, were they dependable. During the big storm of 95, it broke down though, and we called the local Garage. Jali was nice enough to come over right away, with his son, to fix it. After that we learned enough to mostly service it ourselves. Well, we tried.

On one side of the house was an alcove the generator fit in just right, and because it was under an overhang of the house, it wasn't as loud to us in the house as it could have been. Conveniently, this spot was just on the other side of the wall of our laundry room, where Rick had set up shelves to hold the boat batteries, charger, and inverter. We decided early on that Rick would be responsible for electrical things and I would be responsible for plumbing things and that worked well for us. He made a hole in the wall so he could get the generator power cables inside the house to our charger and refrigerator. The generator was not connected to the house power.

Our computers and certain lights throughout the house were always plugged into the inverter. The inverter got it's power from the batteries. The batteries got their power from the charger. The charger got it's power from the house, so everything was always fully charged.

When the power went out, we didn't have to do anything right away, we could run our lights and devices for up to 16 hours on the batteries. Then we would start the generator, unplug the charger from the house power, and plug it into the generator power. We found the five gallon gas tank ran the generator for approximately eight hours, with a full load.

The generator charged up the batteries at night while it also ran the refrigerator, which was sufficient for keeping all our frozen food frozen, and cold food cold. This system provided a constant back up for our computers, which were never running on house power, so they could not be destroyed by power surges, so common in the country. This system kept us going for 20 years.

The longest we went without power was two weeks during the el nino storms of 97/98. Our generator system did not have the power to run the hot water heater, so we had cold showers that whole time. Everyone in Big Sur was without power for the first week, but then the power went back on for most everyone, including us. But as we were cheering the return of power, we watched as a dried out redwood frond was picked up by a wind gust, floated down from the treetops, and landed across both wires of the transformer on our power pole. It sparked, and went dark for another week.

During this time, PG&E had an automated system to report power outages, and for some reason, they thought my report was an anomaly, and they cleared it every time I called. I ended up calling the Big Sur Station, to see if they could help me, and they really did, contacting PG&E on my behalf. Our power was on by the end of the day! Mostly during big storms, the power went out for just one to three days. Our system was just fine for that. We only lost one fridge full of food, it was our extra fridge, and that was our fault for forgetting to plug it in to the generator.

Too Much Stuff

The first mistake we made moving to Big Sur was we brought too much stuff. Stuff that turned out to be useless in the wild environment. I had too many business clothes and not enough clothes for the woods, our tools were skimpy things meant to work on houses that didn't need work. Projects we thought we'd have time to finish now that we were living alone in the woods, they stayed in boxes that eventually got moldy from the moisture in the environment and were thrown out. But getting rid of things in the woods can be difficult and costly.

We had arranged to have regular trash pick-up, once a week on Thursday morning. This was done by the county, and was the only service they provided. We had to have our trash cans out by 6am. We were fine doing that on Wednesday night, we thought. But we didn't yet have a truck, and it's difficult to push heavy trash cans, even wheeled cans, along a dirt path, then over a 175 foot bridge, then up a very steep, partially paved driveway.

The first time we did this we were pretty happy with ourselves that we were able to do it at all, it was way harder than we expected. And we did it the night before. On Thursday morning we went up there to collect our empty trash cans and were shocked to see our empty cans surrounded by four large brown bags full of trash and garbage. Somebody else's garbage. We had no idea that would happen. But it happened every time we put our cans out there.

To resolve this problem, our friendly and helpful neighbors, an adorable couple who had a giant golden retriever, told us about two local businesses who would remove trash for us, but only Marty was willing to drive across the river to get it, so we went with him. Heaven! And he was more reliable than we were. And multi-tasking. He had his fingers in many pies, as his business brought him into contact with just about everybody in Big Sur. He did us a huge favor one time in 1995, after a really big storm. I'll tell you more about that later, but for now, let's just agree that the people who haul away our trash are of the most important people in our lives.

If you haul your own trash to the dump, be proud of yourself. I've driven a raised 4x4 pick-up overflowing with trash, across the river and 50 miles to the dump. That is serious business. The dump in Monterey is the best dump EVER! Everything you dump there gets picked through by the crew and the valuables are taken to the dump's very own second-hand store, recyclables are recycled, and green waste is composted. You can buy the best things there, 80 gallon pickle drums to be used for rain barrels, sinks with faucets and counter tops already attached, as many black garden pots as you can use. You can buy wood chips, colored chips, garden fill, potting soil and compost. Such a sensible way to deal with trash.

Marty only worked for us a few years, though. Then we got our own 4x4 and did it ourselves. Doing this just once will fill you with respect for your own trash hauler. Now I know, the beauty of any area is directly connected to how often the trash is hauled away.

But trash can't be hauled away at certain times, like when the road is closed because it has washed away in a storm, or the water is so high the river can't be crossed by truck. During those times you need to have a way to store your trash, maybe for months. And months. One time we had so much trash, we covered it with a 20 x 20 foot camo mesh tarp. It was so well hidden our guests never suspected they were walking by such an enormous pile of trash. You have to be good at getting rid of garbage so animals don't become a problem. We found a garbage disposal was really helpful, whereas composting kitchen waste attracted animals. We had 18 trash cans when we moved out, half for recycling, half for trash.

Rex the Electronic Dog

After a few years, we installed an electronic dog to watch over our trash, to keep skunks and raccoons out. We had experimented with a few of these electronic devices, in an effort to both scare animals off our trash and keep deer out of the garden, but Rex was the only one to sound real. It sounds like a Doberman barking, a mad Doberman. We attached it to a very good outside speaker, and it worked well. Once we installed that dog, we never had an animal in our trash. Only rodents. We loved Rex.

So did the newest member of our family, our little black and white, terrier/chihuahua mix, who was named Vito by his foster family. We told people that Vito was our Italian dog, that he was a "friend of ours." Vito listened carefully to Rex, and soon we could hear him trying to imitate Rex. It took him some time, but within a year he could bark as deeply as Rex, and he even imitated the growl Rex makes in the middle of his routine. We often recognize the recording of Rex's barking in movies and TV, we know it so well. But Vito, the 12 pound dog, fooled everyone, and between Vito and Rex, it sounded like we had big dogs guarding our place. Even our neighbors were surprised to find Rex was electronic and Vito tiny. They thought we had gotten big dogs.

Living Without Broadcast, Cable or Satellite

One of the big issues we had to consider about moving to Big Sur was not having access to broadcast or cable entertainment or news on television or radio. Our new house had no broadcast TV, as no broadcast waves were able to reach the coastal area, no cable TV, as it's too expensive to run the wires for cable. We had no satellite because the valley the house sits in is so steep and covered with trees, there is no clear line-of-sight access to make a dish useful.

There was a lot of discussion with just about everyone who came to the house about climbing a big Redwood and putting a dish at the top. It always sounded so simple, but after we lived there for a few months, we found the folly in putting a dish high in a tree, and were glad no one convinced us to pay them to do it.

Early on we had a wind event at the coast where 100 mile an hour winds were clocked. We were home, and that really freaked us out. A lot of branches and duff hit the roof, and it was noisy for hours. Big branches, 20 feet long and four or five inches in diameter, loud enough to make us look up, expecting the branch to break through the roof. I jumped out of the way a few times, just in case. The noise made me want to run out of the house to safety, but I was clearly safer in the house with the big, thick roof.

Upstairs, through the clerestory windows, we could see the treetops blowing around violently, and that's when we said, almost simultaneously, "What are we doing here?" But downstairs, looking at the bottom 50 feet of the trunks of the same trees, they weren't moving at all. Unfortunately, the satellite dish would have to be mounted at the tree top to get line of sight, and would have moved around way too much to get reception. We never did get satellite service there.

We could get am radio and cell phone service outside the house, but never inside. Never, ever inside. We couldn't get a GPS reading there either. We used to joke that we could sell the house to some organization who wanted to make sure they couldn't be bugged, like the Mob, CIA or NSA. It was pretty annoying, but another conversation starter.

When we bought the property, we were newlyweds and had very little time for TV, but we were seriously disappointed that we couldn't get a good radio station for music. My husband was a computer programmer for a game company, and he worked so many hours there was little time left for TV or movies. I had just quit a demanding job because I wanted to be able to work from home, too, and had started classes for graphic design so I could.

Our daily habits did not involve watching any particular show. I had been listening to all the news I needed to hear on the radio, in the car on the way to and from work and school, but the one TV fix I really needed was to be able to watch Columbo while I paid the bills. Since I had already seen most of the Columbo shows, because I love Peter Falk, I could keep up with the story while I worked, but still be distracted enough by the show to not worry so much about money while I wrote the checks.

You see, I'm a Professional Worrier, a true expert, tops in my field, and only a professional such as myself knows how to worry so *densely*, that I must use distraction techniques to protect myself against spontaneous collapse of the "worry artery," for which there is no stent. For my protection, in the month we had to pack, Rick set up our VHS recorder to copy as many Columbo episodes as he could. He also copied stand-up comedy from late-night UHF broadcasting. And that was pretty much the only entertainment we had for a few years. About 15 tapes.

These tapes had all the commercials, too, which was annoying in the beginning, but became more entertaining later on, depending on whether the products were still available or not. Back then, people did not want to watch short videos over and over again, that's what commercials on television forced us to do, and everybody wanted out of that experience. The broadcast TV experience we gave up is different from what's available today, with Amazon, Netflix, YouTube, imgur, Roku, and streaming.

Our habits at the time did not include having the TV on every day anyway, so giving up broadcast was not that difficult. We had so much to talk about as a young couple, and especially after we got to Big Sur, TV just wasn't that important. I know there were times in my life when it was very, very, important. I think times I was working too many hours were times I needed TV. I think there's value in that.

Rick's mother made recordings of some shows for us, so we were able to watch Twin Peaks and she copied more Columbo for me, and that was really fun for us, having been deprived for so long. But the tapes she made had sound quality issues and weren't re-watchable. My brother-in-law, a technical wizard, kindly made tapes for us, too, perfect copies of 6 Feet Under and other shows we loved, and it was a real treat. But that was it for a while, until VHS tapes started to show up on sale. When movies were first available on VHS, they were priced for rental stores to buy them to rent out to the public. One copy of a movie would cost $60 to $100. We were not interested in paying that for one movie, we would rather read a book.

The first few years, that's pretty much what we did. At first, I mostly read field guides, histories and information about the natural world around us. Without the Internet, I couldn't just do a search to find out what that bird or bug or flower was. We wanted to know everything we could about our environment. That's why we were there, to spend time learning about the natural world, to balance out our overly technical working life.

AOL was just beginning, and all Internet access was through dial-up modems and was sooo slow. We had three land lines, although they were just called "phone lines" then. Two of the phone lines had modems, so we could each dial-up email, get to whatever Internet was available, and Rick could be on the phone to his office, too.

The biggest search engine at the time was Alta Vista. Google had not yet been heard from. People didn't have websites yet, they had "Home Pages." If you needed to know something, you had to find it yourself in a book, or call an expert to ask. The Internet wasn't yet fleshed out as the "Information Highway" we all know now.

I read about every bird, animal, bug, rodent, amphibian, fish and plant we found. We spent a lot of money in the Nature Conservancy stores and Kepler's Books, collecting field guides. We still have all those field guides, 20 feet of shelf space devoted to those guides. And another five feet of how-to books, another 10 feet on gardening. And we still use them, some more than others, of course. We even have a field guide for freshwater fish, the only field guide we have that also includes recipes for cooking the guide subject. We have a field guide on Slugs and one on Poison Oak and Ivy. We have a field guide on Cows and another on scat (animal poo). We even have a guide to pooping in the woods.

But none of this really answers the question, "How do you live without TV?" By making your own life so interesting that watching TV would take time away from it. That sounds simple, but it's not. I think you have to be curious to find life interesting; I've met people who are not curious, and they need to be entertained by very exciting things.

Habit plays a big role. TV is made to be addicting, but it's also insulting, and then maddening that it's still addicting even though you're insulted. But the thing that, to me, makes the most difference in not having TV is not having TV news and commentary, and videos of news. To this day, I have only seen three videos of the 9/11 events in New York City. All three times I burst into tears.

I stay pretty well informed by reading. I read articles in both right-wing and left-wing news sites, and articles from news organizations and from blogs. I try to read what the extremists on both sides say, as well as what moderates say. Non-sensible info stands out after checking out all sides. Even in the early days of the Internet, it was pretty easy to keep informed without TV news, and I've become better informed by reading more and depending on video less. It leaves my mind more free to also think my own thoughts.

When I read about news events, I can take it at my own pace and re-read if I don't get it. But with video news, even if I don't understand it, I'm fed an attitude about it, and left with their sound bites and images, like it or not. Images fill up my head with images, not thoughts. We don't question the images the news presents to us because we saw it with our own eyes. Maybe it's just easier for me to disengage from the written word and keep my thoughts whole while I still investigate the story.

My feeling about TV, though, is that most folks watch TV for the same reasons, for distraction, for company and a sense of connection to the outside world. We are a gregarious people, even if we just want to be home alone.

Early on we subscribed to TV Guide, even though we couldn't use it, just so we would be able to know what our friends were talking about when we saw them. Eventually, every movie went on sale for $3 to $5 on VHS tape, which is when I would buy them. Then TV shows came out on tape, and I was able to buy the Columbo episodes, and watch them without commercials, a real treat.

We had a price limit for video we tried to never go over. We would get a movie a year or two after it came out. We watch movies more than once. As DVD's took over, our collection changed, too, and now we have more DVD's than we ever had tapes. We gave our tapes to nursing homes years before we moved out of Big Sur. And we thinned out our DVD collection with these guidelines - comedies and mysteries are re-watchable if you wait long enough between watching, and although we watch historical dramas multiple times, we don't watch regular dramas a second time, so we don't buy them.

And now that we live in the suburbs again, and have access to every kind of way to watch TV, we did not get broadcast or cable TV. We bought a Roku and signed up for NetFlix, and Hulu. And that is much more entertainment than we use, as the TV is still not on every day, and we still read the news instead of watch. Reading is pretty important to both of us.

That's why I'm really grateful to the book buyers at Costco. I was already shopping there, so looking through their books was an easy way to keep up with current titles. Their selection has been excellent and included offerings for the whole political and religious spectrum. We started to read books about history when we moved to Big Sur. It seemed only natural. We're still touring the world, reading histories about Egypt, Russia, China, Britain, US, Africa, etc. The world is a big place and history is still happening, so our interest continues. This has been extremely satisfying reading. And there will always be a history book we haven't yet read to capture our attention.

There was another thing we did inside the house to entertain ourselves, and that was to get naked and give each other haircuts.

Internet Access Evolution

We finally went to Verizon for Internet access but it was, as Rick said, "clinging to the Internet by our fingernails." Our last system there used a 2G USB Verizon cellular "dongle," which was placed in the only spot we could find to get high speed reception. Unfortunately, that was outside the house, so we hid it in a decorative hose box. We had the dongle connected to a laptop inside the hose box. The laptop was connected by Ethernet cable to a wireless router, which was directly under the porch roof of the shed outside our house. We connected to that router with the wifi on our laptops, from inside the house.

We didn't have very good reception, though, so to get this system working, Rick drove the dongle and laptop up to the Post Office, where he got good enough reception to register the dongle with Verizon. Then, at home it got nearly good enough reception most of the time, with occasional bursts of speed we never knew how long would last, before coming to a crawl again. Everyone who lives in the country deals with Internet problems like this on a regular basis. It is not convenient.

This system was remarkably stable, all things considered. We used the earliest ad blockers, because downloading news articles with commercials and pictures would slow us down unbearably. We used Linux exclusively; as privacy nerds, we could not accept Microsoft's decree that they would have to be able to access our computers so they could see if we had any stolen software on it. We knew we didn't. But more importantly, who in their right mind would allow any company access to the private files on their computers?

Six Inches in Six Hours

That's a lot of rain. And in 1995, forecasting was not the computer-model driven, almost precise, forecasts we have today, so it was kind of a surprise. A bridge washed out north of us in that storm, a bridge over the Carmel River, and we were stuck in Big Sur for weeks, unable to get supplies. But that storm brought the river up higher and faster than any other time in the 21 years we were there, and some of those years were pretty powerful el ninos. We had two storms, in 2010 and 2012, that dropped 10 inches in 24 hours, and in neither case was the river as high as it was in the six inches in six hours storm. A lot has to do with soil saturation and high tide and how much water is already in the river.

When the tide is high, water in the river can't empty as fast into the ocean as it can when the tide is low. When soils are still absorbing rainwater, not as much of the rain makes it into the rivers. If the soils are fully saturated, then all the rain goes right into the rivers. So a big storm early in the year usually doesn't cause as much flooding trouble as a big storm later in the year, after it's been raining a lot and the soils can't absorb any more.

After seeing the changes wrought by this storm and the power of fast moving water from this really big storm, I came to have an intense interest in the inch-per-hour rate. Now I have computer accuracy available, back then, I had a five inch rain gauge that I had to watch closely enough that I would know when it would reach five inches, so I could empty it, in case we had more than that in one storm. My first gauge was a dinky little thing that I couldn't even see from inside the house, so after this storm, when I first fully understood just how important this information was to our safety, I got a giant thing with a large, neon yellow float in a tube two feet high. It's pretty visible. But it still only measured five inches before I had to go out and dump out the water and get it back in it's stand again, which was never easy, and usually involved getting drenched from rain. Weather stations with computer counting of rain drops were not yet readily available.

The night of the big storm, we had hunkered down. We were not expecting so much rain, but still, we had seen six inches in 24 hours before, and the river never even got close to the house; near, yeah, but not close. We were busy working on a project that night, so we weren't watching closely and didn't know the possible danger until someone from the fire department called at 11pm. We were pretty shocked by that in itself, then the guy asked us if our bridge was still up. By this time, I was getting better at staying calm in the face of adversity, but that question sent fear coursing through my body. I laughed nervously and said I was too afraid to look. He said we should definitely go look and call him back if it wasn't still up. I remember thinking, "What do you mean, 'not still up? How hard has it been raining?"

So we got into our rain gear and went outside. We wanted to circle the house before we went to the bridge. The river was roaring so loudly, louder than we had heard before, loud enough that we had to scream to hear each other even when we were right next to each other. When we aimed our flashlights on what was usually a terraced path, one foot down from the house level, we saw water moving by and it was moving fast, *fast*. This was just eight feet from the corner of the house, water closer than we'd ever seen. Just standing next to the raging river felt more dangerous than any other storm, and we'd already been through a drought busting el nino. But the bridge was still standing, and we found no problems that needed attention, so we went back to watch the house.

Then the hard rain stopped abruptly, like a faucet had been turned off, and the river emptied quite a bit overnight. When we went outside the next day, we were once again overwhelmed by nature's force and beauty. What we found on the far bank of the river was a rock wall that was more than 4 feet tall, 3 feet wide and 60 feet long; it straddled our driveway and completely blocked us from driving across the river. The wall looked as if it had been professionally laid, the top was so flat and all the rocks were so tightly fit together. The precision was astounding. The side facing the river was perfectly vertical, so polished, it was exquisitely done. We were blown away by the power of the river, that water could have built that high a wall, that straight and flat topped. It was bright and beautiful.

In some areas, the bank on our side of the river had been transformed as well and had sand deposited that was nearly as high as the rock wall, while other areas seemed to just have a foot or two more of sand. We talked about this storm a lot. The changes were so drastic and literally overnight. We thought what happened was the extra amount of rain falling so quickly made the river run fast and deep, digging a deep channel down the center of the river, and forcing what had been the bottom of the river, off to the sides, out of the way of the rushing water. Seems like when the rain stopped abruptly, the rocks that were being carried along by the speed and force of the water dropped pretty much where they were, forming the rock wall, and sandy bank opposite.

It was just a guess, and there wasn't, at the time, a way to find out if we were correct. But not long after that, we read an article in a science magazine reporting on studies done on the Rio Grande, where they could set the rate of water flow from the dam to test this, and proved that a fast moving river deposits more sand on the banks than a slow moving river.

The parts of the river that didn't change as much were out of the way of the major rush of water down the center. We saw a big area up stream that had been damned years before by storms and had became a swimming hole off to the side of the river. In this storm, the swimming hole was filled in with sand when the water was high and moving fast, and then as the river emptied, it built an angled sand wall at that bank, because the water was moving slower on that side of the river as it went around a bend.

Part of the beauty of this event was from the fast moving water scrubbing the rocks clean of all algae and bug eggs, revealing granite rock colors of brilliant white, white/gray, white/gray/black, reddish garnet rocks, and blue-green serpentine rocks with white streaks through them. The rock wall was mostly out of the water, just off to the side of the main flow, on the outside bend of the river. Along the entire river bottom, every rock was sparkling clean and bright, making it easier to see everything going on in the water. This made the entire river area brighter, as every bit of sun that made it to the river was reflected all around. Even the trees on the banks were brightened.

River Bottom Sequence of Events

A moment here to talk about the river bottom - There is a sequence of events that form the environment of the river bottom. It starts with a hell of a storm, a storm with so much rain falling, the river runs really fast and washes the rocks clean of all algae and bug eggs. And not just from the speed of the water, but from the sand the water is carrying, sandblasting the rocks clean. After that, the black biting flies get the first real estate on the rocks in spring.

Female flies have laid their eggs in the water, at the edges where the water flows slower. The eggs hatch into larvae, who have suction cups at one end. Somehow, through cold water moving fast enough to carry a lot of oxygen, these tiny beings find their way to rocks and attach themselves with that suction cup (field guides say suction disk) to the rocks. While there, the larvae filter feed on bacterias and diatoms and very tiny particles. When they're ready, they pupate in cocoons that are also attached by suction disk to rocks. When they're done with that, they break out and float in an air bubble to the surface, and fly away. These tiny flies feed on nectar and the females bite for blood so they can make eggs. And they're pretty much everywhere in Big Sur in spring and summer. We quit wearing white or light colors in spring and summer there in the woods, or we'd be covered with flies. I quit smelling white flowers, too, after I got a bunch of flies up my nose. Ugh!

As summer wears on, the rocks become more and more covered with these different stages of bug life, and algae starts to grow, too. At this point, the rocks look hairy, and they're slippery to walk on. This coating of algae and bug life continues to get thicker and thicker every year, and more and more slippery until there is another huge storm to wipe everything clean. And the cycle begins again.

We were still in awe of the rock wall and the power of the river when Marty, the kind man who was removing our trash every other week offered to remove the rocks and clear a path for driving across the river again. All he wanted in return was the rocks. We were so grateful. It seemed like a perfect deal to us, and what community was all about. He was building a rock wall for someone else in Big Sur, and collecting rock we didn't know what to do with saved him from having to make multiple, 100 mile round trips to purchase them.

And since he was the one driving across the river to collect our trash, he filled in the deep channel that had been dug out by the fast moving water, by having his guys toss one rock at a time into the channel until it was filled in and was flat enough to drive cross. It took a whole day. And that's how we learned what to do to make it possible to drive across the river in summer and fall. We did that job every July for 17 years. Even though that work was difficult, back-breaking work that sometimes took three days to do and at least that long to recover from, it's one of the things I miss most about living in Big Sur. No matter how hard the work, being in the river was more fun than the work was hard. Feeling the current of the water as you work is almost like a massage, and when everything you see is interesting, it's a mental massage as well. The full spa treatment, so to speak.

By late July or August, the water was low enough to get in and work, and the temperature of the air was warm enough to find being in the cold water refreshing, well usually. We used our hands in leather gloves, a rounded-tip shovel and a digging bar, if we had to move really big rocks. Some years we only had to toss rocks small enough that we could toss them, into small holes. Other years we had to work harder and move bigger rocks into bigger holes.

For about five years there were giant boulders on the "fast side" of the riverbank, then one year, after one big storm, they were gone. There were rocks everywhere, of course, we didn't have to go more than a few feet up or down river to collect rocks that were loose on the river bottom or bank of the river. Then carry them back and drop them into holes. We didn't take rocks that exposed the sandy bottom.

However strong you are when you start this work, the work makes you stronger. Walking through four feet of water, up and downstream, carrying rocks is harder than it sounds. (I come from pretty hardy stock, though. My Dad was riding his motorcycle through his town on his 75th birthday, and he said "some old coot" ran a red light and crashed into him, and Dad was so mad about that because he hurt his knee, and could no longer remove and replace a transmission by himself.)

We always checked the area before we started working, checked for anything living in the rocks we wanted to move or in the holes we were filling. We never found anything. Once we saw a small crawdad floating towards us from up stream, dead, on it's back and my dog Buddy snapped that up quick. But I think the way two river channels converged at the driveway made it an undesirable place for river life to want to be, the currents too difficult to navigate. Probably the same forces that made us have to fill in the trench ever year.

A few years in, a young local guy wanting to start his life came by to ask if we minded if he took a big redwood log, one that was part of a log jam upstream from our house, so he could mill it up and build himself a place to live in. We told him it wasn't our log or our land and so we couldn't say anything one way or the other. No one claimed ownership of the log. He removed it and did such a clean job of it, we couldn't tell how he got it out, we could only see that it was gone. We were impressed.

What does that have to do with needing to fill in our driveway? Well, the log was a large diameter log and it had been blocking the passage of water through a side channel, so that channel filled up with water only when the river was flowing high enough to get over that six foot tall logjam. It didn't happen that often. The side channel emptied just at our driveway, and the two channels of water meeting up there usually carved a trench on the house side, the very trench we got stuck in when moving in.

Once the log was removed, the water always came through that channel, and every year in winter the river dug out the rocks we worked so hard to put in the trench the previous July. I wouldn't exactly say I looked forward to doing that job, but once in the water, I couldn't help but love it. I thought I would miss the redwoods the most, but I was wrong about that, too. I miss the river most of all. I miss the sound, the flora and fauna, the activity, the ever-changing, always interesting scenery, the life-bringing wetness of water.

Watching the color of the river water clear up from dark brown to light brown, to dirty green, to a beautiful, pale jade green, and seeing the rocks reveal themselves through the water is one of the very special natural things you look forward to, like wildflowers, and robins in spring. A very special sight that doesn't happen every year, you know you're lucky if you get to see it.

What's Different About Rural Living?

Coming from the suburbs, I didn't really understand the enormous difference living rurally would make in my life. I had lived in San Francisco for more than a year once, and besides dealing with more people and traffic, having to pay almost as much for my parking space as for my studio apartment was the biggest difference I found between city and suburb.

But the biggest differences between living an urban lifestyle and living a rural lifestyle have to do with people, jobs, dirt, noise, bugs, running water, and most of all, self reliance and supplies. You might think wild animals would be on this list, but suburban folks deal with almost as much wildlife as we did.

Rural life is hard. It's hard to make friends when everyone lives an hour apart, over country roads. There aren't enough businesses, jobs, doctors or dentists. There is usually a lot of dirt. There is a lot less noise (unless you have a pellet stove.) There are a lot of bugs. A lot. Every house has it's own water system in the country, and is it's own source of unique problems. There are always trips for supplies, paired with very little public transportation, so you need good vehicles, and good friends.

We moved there thinking we wanted to protect trees, but ended up carrying a chainsaw in the trunk of the car. If a tree falls across traffic in the city or suburbs, everybody has to wait or find a detour. Only approved people can do the jobs. In the country, there is no alternative route, and many of the folks blocked by a fallen tree have a chainsaw in their trunk. They hop out of their cars, get to work immediately and often have a path cleared before services arrive. When you're in the country, services may never arrive. Folks in the country have learned not to wait, they want to solve their own problems.

When we had to have our kitchen wall rebuilt, and then finally installed kitchen cabinets in the kitchen, I did dishes outside, in front of the house, for four months. I had a plastic garden-sink-cabinet that I put a high, kitchen faucet on. I connected it to a hose I already had for washing the dogs outside, and turned the hot water up. I let the gray-water out on a big pile of redwood chips, and I added a table on each side of the sink for dish-washing flow. It was great!

I would say that was the very best dish-washing experience I've ever had, or ever will have. It still makes the list of top nature experiences I've had, even though I can't call out any particular event. I put the sink out far enough from the house that I had a great view of the river, and could see all around me, and watch the action while I stood outside doing dishes. I enjoyed it so much, the longer I did it, the slower I did it. I did that from October through January, and when it started raining, we put an outside umbrella up, covered it with a tarp and hung up a lamp. I wore a fleece vest, and my hands were in warm water, so I was warm, too. I don't think you could do that in the suburbs. That's a country thing.

Winter Supply

The first thing we needed to do in our new house was get a load of wood for the wood burning stove, the only source of heat on the property. We estimated we would need five cords of wood just for the winter. We thought we had over-estimated, just in case we needed more than the three cords locals suggested. We needed more. Much more.

Even though keeping warm with a wood stove seemed so romantic, it turns out it's really an unpaid, part-time job, and there will be no slacking off on this job! It takes time, you can't just turn the thermostat up. We had to walk to the wood pile. We had to have gloves to shoo the spiders and rodents away, and not get splinters. To bring in enough wood for the day, we needed a cart of some kind, and then a place to put the wood before it gets into the stove. And something to cover the cart with so the wood doesn't get wet on the way into the house.

The wood has to be cut the right length for the stove, if it's too long, which our second order was, you won't be able to fit it in the stove. Some mistakes you only make once, and that one qualifies. The stove has to be cleaned regularly, and the chimney has to be cleaned which means you can't use the stove while it cools down, either. It's an endless trudge. We found it took a minimum of four hours of labor every day to keep the house warm. Between the building of fires and the cleaning of ashes, the burn holes, the smoke, the chimney, I hope I will never have to use a wood burning stove again. I don't want to.

But that first year was a doozy of learning and not just on how to build a good fire. We learned the hard way, of course. We moved in at the end of September, it started raining the day after Thanksgiving, and didn't stop until the end of June. The river didn't get low enough to cross until October of the next year, and we were worried it would start raining again before we could get our next load of wood. We had spent the better part of the year carrying boxes of wood over the bridge, one box at a time. Very expensive. We knew if we bought by the cord and had it stacked by our cars, it would be stolen.

That first year brought a new term to my awareness, "Winter Supply." It would come to take over my life. The whole time we lived in Big Sur, we found it best to have enough of certain things we would need for an entire year, before the start of rain. More on that later. For two more years we burned wood, and got 10 cords of wood delivered and stacked for us, just before first rain.

We soon traded the beautiful and romantic wood stove for the convenience of a noisy pellet stove. They don't mention the noise when they sell it to you, that's a secret surprise. When the thermostat turns the stove on, the auger turns noisily to drop pellets into the bowl to burn, and you can hear every pellet hit the bottom of the bowl, all night long. Then a loud fan. But the convenience of not building a fire was so great that we loved that pellet stove anyway. We used the wood-to-pellet stove conversion charts (we guessed) and decided we needed eight tons of pellets. So how to get eight tons of pellets (400 bags, 40 lbs each) across the river and ready to use every year?

To help us out, my father brought us a 1983 Ford 150 ½ ton truck that was raised up, and being the "body and fender man" he was, he also welded together a trailer from the bed of another truck. The truck itself had the biggest tire-flaps in the back I'd ever seen, and folks stopped us all the time to ask why we had them. We didn't know, but it was always fun chatting with people about the possibilities.

With that set-up, though, I could go to Orchard Supply Hardware (OSH) and buy a whole ton of pellets, and they would load them in the truck and trailer for me. But it was difficult to get the truck and trailer down the driveway, across the river, then back up hill to the house on the unpaved driveway. So I mostly got a half ton and went to OSH 16 times between when we could cross the river and first rain. Yeah, that didn't last long, just 10 years or so.

We found the locals at Blaze Engineering were willing to pick up the pellets for us and even stack them in our shed for a very reasonable price. It meant they could make money on their way back home, when they would usually have had an empty truck making no money. So we did that for a couple years before the Load Handler changed our lives.

A Load Handler is a very slippery piece of Kevlar-like material that lines a truck bed. Your load goes on top of the material. There is a crank handle to use that rolls the material up like a roller shade, at the end of the tailgate, which pulls the load to the tailgate. That way you never have to get into the bed of the truck and bend over to empty it, you can stand at the tailgate and crank it out, instead. I could go to OSH, buy a ton of pellets, get half of it loaded on the load handler, drive home, cross the river to the shed, crank a row of bags of pellets to the tailgate, and unload them myself. I could, but Rick always helped unload and stack. Then I'd go back and we'd do it again. We'd do that every other day until all eight tons were stacked. That's a lot of work to stay warm. Looking back, I don't know why we didn't just pick up a bag of pellets and carry them around the house till we were warm, it would have been so much less trouble, and cheaper, too.

The Load Handler helped when I took trash to the dump, too, and that was always fun. When you get to the dump there, you are told to do a 3-point back-up to the spot you dump your load. There are trucks lined up next to each other while unloading. I'm just 5'1", 100 lbs, so when I hopped out of my raised truck to unload, I usually got lots of snickers and not very nice comments from the guys unloading nearby. My load was usually overflowing, and only once did a guy ask if I needed help. But I didn't. I would remove my cover tarp, lower my tailgate, get my crank handle, and empty the entire load in seconds. I'd smile and wave goodbye to the guys that snickered the most, while they were still standing in the back of their trucks, still emptying their load. Always fun.

Getting supplies so we could stay warm was the first way we created our winter supply. Being prepared for disaster started with first aid. We were 25 miles away from a drug store, we couldn't just run to the pharmacy when we had a need. That would take at least an hour and a half of driving, not something you want to do when you don't feel well, or are bleeding from cutting yourself on a tool. We had to already have that stuff at home. So I started to collect first aid equipment: band-aids, every kind of ointment and cream, ice packs, snake bite kit, antiseptic wash, cough drops, cough syrup and of course, alcohol and hydrogen peroxide, and skunk odor wash. All of this stuff has to be replaced every few years, when you find the band-aids won't stick anymore.

We had enough gas cans to have as much as 40 gallons of gas on hand, for eight days without power. We tried to keep 10 gallons at all times. Then if the power went out, we would high-tail it up to the gas station at Ripplewood, where they had a generator and could still pump gas, and fill up the rest of the cans. Only once in 21 years did we have power out longer than a week. But the power went out All. The. Time.

Enough tea and coffee for a year? We found a coffee bean roaster willing to sell us 25 lbs of great coffee, and ship it for free. I'd vacuum-seal that up in five lb bags and keep all but one in the outside fridge. And after 2006, I was able to get 12 boxes of Tetley Tea shipped, which lasted me an entire year.

Every year we replaced a large container of powdered milk that had .5% milk-fat and could make 33 gal. of milk. Powdered milk doesn't have a long shelf life, especially the kind with added milk-fat. I can't live without milk and Cheerios, so we had lots of large boxes of cereal, too. When we were stuck at home, or even just sick, we could dip into these stores and not have to leave the house.

We had enough meat frozen to last at least 6 months and both canned and frozen veggies to last at least that long, too. So while I would replace the powdered milk and rice only once a year, we were always depleting and refreshing certain stocks, like Cheerios. They don't last long and you can't have a years supply of them.

The other difficulty was keeping enough prescription meds on hand. Insurance companies will not allow you to buy enough to have extra for winter or emergency supply, so we had to pay full price for these meds, and get doctors' approval to have the extra drugs on hand. This is maddening, all government instruction on how to survive a disaster calls for the public to have these extra medications, but there isn't a program to allow us do it.

I don't know how, but I kept the winter supply inventory all in my head, and only made lists before shopping. Oh, the shopping! I put a giant cooler in the back of the car so I could buy six gallons of non-fat milk for drinking, and two gallons of 2% for coffee and tea, and once in a while, half-and-half. We kept one of each kind of milk in the inside fridge and the rest in the outside fridge.

Once a week or so, off to do a "town run." I had the Forester, and I packed that thing solid when I went shopping. I'd stop at Longs, Orchard Supply Hardware, Target, two different pet stores, Costco and Safeway to get just regular stuff. I'd get home near dark, Rick would connect our two wagons like a train, and bring them both over the bridge to the car. We'd load the groceries in the wagons, and each take one back, over the bridge, to the house and fridge.

We had a few different covers for the grocery wagons when it rained. None of them worked well at all. And we had to use a wagon made of metal mesh, to let the rain fall through. Otherwise, with such a long distance from car to home, we'd end up with grocery soup, no fun at all. It was always an exhausting day for me. I'm tired now just writing about it.

And I hurt myself pulling the wagon, so I asked my Dad to make me a handle I could push the wagon with instead of pull, and I gave him a drawing to use. He's a master welder and he made two handles, and we used them every day till we moved out. That wagon handle was so useful, every worker that came to our house wanted to use it.

The handle allowed me to move 200 to 500 lbs around the place by myself, depending on the wagon body. We had 9 wagons over the years, usually bought two at a time, but once we had those handles, we put them on every wagon we bought. The load was still behind me, but I was pushing it, using my back and thighs. One finally broke, but I still have one of the handles even though I no longer need to use a wagon to get supplies. Living in the suburbs does have it's pleasures.

Water We Doing Here?

It sounded so simple. "Just plug in the pump every three days, before the tank is empty. The pump may look old and decrepit, but it fills the tank, and then all you have to do is unplug it when the tank overflows." How hard can that be? Jerry, who had been renting the cabin, had been doing it for seven years, and he looked healthy, so we thought we could do it too. And we did the hell out of it.

It worked beautifully for two months, during which time we were charmed by knowing exactly where our water came from. It came directly from the river. We could see how clean the water in the river was just by looking out back. We were so impressed, we were obnoxiously giddy about it and ripe for a fall. So many falls. Turns out, keeping water flowing to a unique property has unique opportunities. I think a better word is challenges. I used to have a book with a subtitle that went something like, "If you live in the country, you either have had, will have, or are having trouble with your water supply." Loaned it out and never got it back!

The whole system sure looked simple, though. It had an ancient 500 gallon wooden wine vat now used as a water tank, sitting 25 feet up the hill, to one side of the house, with an ancient pump on the opposite side, between the house and the river. And that was pretty much all we knew and all we had when we moved in.

The pump had an intake pipe that was connected to the river by an 80 foot flexible black hose, with holes around the last two feet of pipe and metal window screening wrapped around that. The end of the pipe was laying in the bottom of the river, balanced on top of some rocks, not just laying in the sand, and the water in the river was so low that the pipe was only about six inches under water. The water was crystal clear, the screening was just to keep fish from being sucked into the pump. But the flaw in this system is using water from the tank to prime the pump. If we accidentally let the tank run dry, which we did all the time, we had to fill the water pipe ourselves, from the big bottles.

The route the water took from the pump to the tank also seemed a bit unusual, but we couldn't think of anything particular about it that would be problematic. There was a garden hose going from the pump to a hose-faucet on the back side of the house, which allowed the water to be pumped through the house plumbing, then up the hill and into the tank. We thought we would be improving the system over time, so we didn't worry about it. We should have.

There was another hose faucet on the side of the house by the tank, and a white PVC pipe went from that faucet, up the hill, to the tank. The pipe continued past a "T" connector at the bottom of the tank that served as the water out, went up the side of the tank and into the top. So the same pipe that filled the tank, emptied the tank, and fed the water into our sinks and tubs. It also fed water back to the pump to prime the pump when we turned it on. It was a most efficient use of piping, and the most unconventional, of course, but we didn't know that yet, and what mattered to us was only that it worked.

It looked like it would fall apart any second, but it did work, we saw it, and apparently it had been working for many years. Looking back, I see that we wanted to believe in magic, we had already drunk the Kool-Aid, when we fell in love with the uniqueness and the Redwoods and the river. We didn't really want to know all the ways our system would come to fail in the future. We had no idea how cold we would be when fixing this system, or how hard it is to keep an eye out for mountain lions while pouring a 5 gallon bottle of water into a small, one inch hole, to fill an 80 foot long, 1 inch diameter pipe, to prime the pump. But man that water was clean!

Then the rain started. After seven years of severe CA drought, it rained so much, way more than we had ever seen before in the suburbs. It was like solid water coming down, it could not be seen through. The water in the river turned so many shades of first green and then brown, we were dumbfounded and mesmerized. I stood at the back sliding door every chance I got, watching the water. Without a doubt, the most surprising color was "chocolate milkshake." The water was so thick with dirt that it was visibly thick, like a milkshake with waves and foam.

And the logs that flew swiftly down the center of the river were shocking. Every possible size, thickness, and length flew by. For the past seven years, trees that fell in the woods had been working their way slowly downhill to the river. And when the river flows higher than it has in many years, the water picks up more of these fallen trees and carries them to the ocean, where they become dangerous missiles that damage boats.

The higher the river got, the more logs went by, some with big branches sticking up that could easily get caught up in our bridge. On the way to the ocean, they get caught up in bends of the river and form dams, or build up behind bridges and form dams that threaten to tear the bridges down and make our roads to safety impassable. This presented a whole new level of concern, a constant concern, really, about our water supply, and safety.

We were sucking up "surface water," which is not potable, which means cleared for drinking, so it needed to be filtered or treated. We found a great counter-top water filter that was gravity fed so it required no power. It was a *ceramic candle* filter, which was originally designed for the Queen of England. It works in two sections, the top has the water filters (up to five filters) in it, and is also where you pour pitchers of water to start the process. The bottom collects the clean water. As far as I know, this is the only kind of filter made for water that is not potable, called "raw" water. Every other water filter, including reverse osmosis, is meant to be used with potable tap water that has already been treated by your city's water supplier. I added a new, and well cleaned, hand-pump garden-sprayer to the kitchen, which I kept filled with filtered water, that we could use to rinse things, like fruit.

Neither of us had spent *any* time on a river before. It seemed more like a creek when we first saw it in June, but winter in California is a whole different animal. That first year, it started to rain the Monday after Thanksgiving, and it seemed to never stop. I believe the total rain for that year was 64 inches at our house. Everyone we talked to said the River hadn't run like that for 10 years.

I heard there was so much rain that year, the road was washed away and it took 18 months to rebuild. I began to prepare for such an event by buying extra: canned goods, bulk foods, dried fruit, nuts, paper supplies, (paper plates, cups and bowls, plastic utensils, tissues, TP, paper towels, we used paper plates when the power was out) soaps, laundry supplies, dark chocolate, baby wipes, tequila, Hennessey's, oranges, turkey jerky and dried mango, gas cans and gas stabilizer. The amounts I kept stored depended on the the NOAA el nino forecast. During el nino, I stocked more of everything.

Seeing the colors change in the river that winter, we had to adjust our water pumping to the times the river was clear enough to pump water we wanted to use. Our only filter was on the counter in the kitchen. Other locals mentioned their own green bath water, so we knew we weren't the only folks using it unfiltered. Some years we used water in the winter as if we were in a drought, even though there was so much water around, everywhere. The year we had 84 inches of rain (97/98), the water was brown so often, I set up a "pee tent" outside.

It was a little pop up tent made to change clothes at the beach or to shower at a campsite. It didn't have a floor, so I could just hide in there to squat and pee on the ground, and not have to flush the toilet so often. I moved the tent around so I wasn't going in the same spot repeatedly. But it was cold, so I only peed outside when I knew it was going to be raining for days on end, and the river would be muddy for a long time. I did notice that guys visiting us rarely asked to use our bathroom, they would just disappear into the woods, happy to look around while taking care of business.

That first year, as the water in the river rose and changed colors, I went shopping, and over the course of the winter bought 30 pairs of underwear and socks for each of us, and enough towels to last a month. I didn't plan to buy that many, it's just that as I couldn't wash any whites in that dirty water, I bought more to use. And it turns out that 30 or so days is the longest I've had to wait to do laundry because the water was too yellow or brown to wash whites. It was less expensive in the long run to have extra clothes than trying to get to a laundromat, especially in the rain when you could get stuck in town by a mudslide, forcing you into a motel for a night, or a month. I still keep 30 days of clothes, it's still convenient.

In January of our first year, there was a big storm with a freeze that lasted three days, an unusual occurrence that effected almost the whole of California. It had been raining a lot, and the water in the river was high and wide, almost up to the pump, and suddenly, it was frozen, too. A whole field of frozen water between us and the water still rushing in the middle of the river. When we tried to turn the pump on, it wouldn't pump water, not a drop.

We had to leave home just then for two days, so we got to our hotel early and showered there. When we came back we found the water had receded and the end of our pipe had disappeared into mud. We put on our boots and tried to pull the pipe out. It seemed like it would be easy since we were sinking in the muddy sand as we neared the pipe, but it wouldn't budge. We called Blaze Engineering, and Nick came out to help us. He used unfiltered river water, too.

He told us in no uncertain terms that we would have to learn how to run the system ourselves, repair the pump, lay pipe, glue connectors, and understand the basics of getting water to flow if we were to survive there in the wilds of Big Sur. He said it was too expensive to call for help every time we would need it, that we would need it often (he was so right about that!) and there aren't enough workers in Big Sur to help everyone who had water troubles in a storm.

Nick said we would need to learn to be self reliant in this and many other ways if we expected to last there on that side of the river. He got the water running, though, after he ran a new intake pipe to the river with a foot valve on it, since the river had completely buried the pipe during the course of the storm. He was a great plumber and his advice was great, too. Just the talking to we needed. It was such good advice, we were too embarrassed to call him again the next time we needed help; but we just hadn't learned enough yet to fix it ourselves.

The plumber we called made plans to come out on a Thursday. When a storm came in that day, we expected him to cancel, but he showed up in a rain suit. He wasn't even local, he was from Wilson's, 50 miles away, a suburban area I passed on my way to the Bay Area. We had asked him to separate the "in to" and "out of" the water tank, so we could have a separate line from the pump to the tank, and the tank to the house, in hopes of never losing a tank of water again. We were prone to losing tanks of water because we had added a timer to the system, you know, so we would always have water.

We'd already had the experience of all the water in the tank draining because the foot-valve in the river lost it's seal, which means a little, tiny piece of sand got stuck in the valve, and kept the valve from closing fully, which let the water slowly leak out of the tank, through the house and the pump, and back down into the river, out the pipe it came in.

To recover, we first had to put on our boots and go down into the river water, to the end of the pipe, and jiggle the flap in the foot valve to release the teeny-tiny piece of sand holding the valve open. Then we had to fill the whole pipe with water up to the pump. That's what they mean by "priming the pump." A pump has to have water in it before it will move the water, and the water has to be continuous from the source to the pump.

It can't have a foot long bubble of air in the pipe somewhere. It's surprising how many gallons of water a little one inch diameter pipe can hold. It's 80 feet of pipe, and as I recall, we had a funnel and 5 five-gallon jugs of water on the bank at all times for when this happened. It happened a lot in the first years. The pipe held 13 gallons, two and a half bottles of water required to prime the pump. Doing this with flash lights, in the cold, and the dark, and the rain, while you ponder the location of the nearest mountain lion, was the price of admission to the ride.

After way too many hours spent priming the pump, we realized we could separate the in and out pipes and never have to prime the pump again. If you're thinking, "Never say never," you'd be right on the money. Reminiscing with my husband today about how naive we were to think, "We'll just add a timer, how simple and perfect is that?" we laughed so hard, we cried.

We wanted the plumber to separate the in and out pipes, add some sort of a sediment catch on the system so we could reduce the sediment in the water we were pumping uphill, and we wanted a way to see if the pump was actually pumping water without having to go around the house, climb the hill, and listen for the water. There was no valve to open near the pump to check. Oh yeah, and we wanted a new toilet and new faucets installed in the bathroom sinks, too. We thought it would take days. He did it all that day, during the hardest rain I had ever seen, and left by 6:30. He is still a hero to me.

He had to lay PVC pipe from the pump to the tank, gluing the pieces together in the rain, putting them under a deck, 60 feet up a very steep hill and into the tank. He had to cut each piece to fit the lay of the land on the hill. We didn't want to disturb the hillside and possibly cause a mini-mudslide by digging a ditch up a hill. We thought the duff that falls from the Redwoods almost year round would cover the pipe quickly enough. (We were wrong about that. It took about ten years to cover a white pipe with naturally falling duff on a hill; conversely, it takes just one gust of wind to forever cover a prized tool mistakenly left outside.) The poor guy had to work on his knees in the rain, on a hill and it was raining so hard, at times we couldn't see him.

Since that time I have laid quite a bit of PVC pipe myself, gluing the pieces together, and this sounds easy, but I've found it requires strength and diligence for a long line. Cutting the pipe properly, getting the gluing right so there are no leaks, while not getting any on the ground in our sensitive environment is no easy task. He shielded his work from the rain with a big hat, and used paper towels under the connections to keep the glue from hitting he ground. He used special glue that works in the rain. I learned how to do it that day, by watching that guy. He was amazingly pleasant the entire time and did everything right! He installed major parts of our system that were still in use 21 years later when we sold the property. I learned so much that day.

It was when the pump died, though, that my true plumbing education began. I had to learn about the pump to be able to replace it, and it was so old that none of the suppliers I knew had ever heard of it, so they couldn't repair it. The pump was so old, there were no plastic parts on it. I wish I had understood how valuable that was, but I was too naive to try harder to get it fixed and kind of panicked about not having water. But I was able to read the specs off the pump, and measure the pipes it was connected to, to find what I needed was a ¾ hp jet-pump with an inch intake opening and an inch output opening. I was able to find that at Orchard Supply Hardware.

I was able to find so much of what we needed for this property at that store, and I got so much good advice from the guys who worked there. I talked with them so much, it felt more like I was visiting friends than shopping. What really surprised me, though, was how much I learned from talking with other customers in the plumbing department. Lots of independent plumbers go there for parts, so there are professionals right there, in the isles. I was younger and blond, and essentially a damsel in distress, and I was lucky enough to get help from many kind plumbers who were curious about what I was doing with those plumbing parts.

One time, there were four different guys in the plumbing pipe isle, and I said loudly, "Excuse me guys, which is the best pipe goop?" Two guys shrugged, but the other two said the same brand, and one of them said it was because when he used the other brand, the water tasted funny. Only someone with experience can offer advice like that. It was talking with other customers in the isles that I came to understand the difference between a shallow well pump and a deep well pump, and to know we needed a shallow well pump.

Over time we came to know that we were doing so many things wrong, according to official plumbing standards and the books we read about plumbing, but our requirements were "unique" and required doing things differently. For instance, the shallow well pumps come in two versions, standard and jet, and we needed the jet because the height and the distance we were moving the water was much higher than they recommend.

But moving up to the next, more powerful pump, a deep well pump, would require replacing the piping on both sides of the pump. Because it draws so much more water at one time, our little 1 inch pipes wouldn't allow enough water to be sucked up to keep the pump wet enough while it runs. It will run dry and burn out in seconds. I know this because I tried to upgrade once. Okay, twice. Well, lets just say that I blew out two pumps before I completely understood how to make water run reliably there. Learning is expensive, whether you pay for an education, or you get educated through failure, I mean experience.

It seemed like every storm, when the river rose, our pipe with the foot valve on the end of it would get buried under sand and rocks, and the sand would compromise the foot valve, after which it would never work reliably again, and after losing a tank or two of water, I'd buy a new one. PVC pipe is pretty flexible, and even though we laid it perpendicular to the river, when the rain swelled the river, it bent the pipe downstream, around some big alders, and buried it. I got tired of having to dig the pipe out of the sand every time it rained, so I decided to put an empty, sealed-and-so-floating, 3-gallon water bottle on the end of the pipe.

I attached it just above the foot valve and with about eight inches of extra rope, which let the foot valve ride eight inches under the surface of the water, under the bottle. It worked really well because the river water clears up by gravity, so the top clears first. You can look at the water and see that the top foot of water is clear, whereas the deeper water is not. I could fill the tank as soon as the foot valve was floating in clear water.

When the river rose more than two feet, the river got wider and caused the bottle and pipe to get hung up on the trees and bushes on the side of the river, and every time, it would lose it's prime. When the water rose really high, the bottle would be held underwater and we'd have to wait till the river went down far enough that our bottle would re-appear. I had to go to the riverbank and disengage the pipe and bottle from whatever debris it had been entangled up in, usually between two and five feet above the standard low water mark, and then put it back in the water.

Our 500 gallon tank really only lasted about two days, so we did a lot of pumping and priming. Just writing about this brings a huge wave of satisfaction over me – we got that water to run in the worst of times, ourselves, using determination, resolve and sometimes the generator. We never hired a plumber to make the water run again, we did it ourselves for 20 years.

My Father's Well-Tip

A few years after we moved in, my father showed up at our house with a well-tip he said would solve all our water problems. A well-tip is essentially a pipe with a point at one end, and a mesh section that allows water to be pulled through, but not sand. He lived in New Jersey, and the well tip was made for use in environments like his – pure sand. He just had to stand it on the ground and hammer it down to use it at his house, but our river has a rocky bottom, so it was more complicated. He refused to believe it would be difficult. I didn't believe it would work, and I wasn't enthusiastic about installing it at all. But he absolutely insisted and there is no arguing with Dad. And it turns we wouldn't have been able to stay there after the Basin fire in 2008 if we hadn't installed it, because the river water was too muddy, for three years, to draw from the surface as we had been doing. It just wasn't pump-able.

The well tip was about 4½ feet tall, with a 90° elbow connector on top. We wanted to install it so the entire tip and the connecting pipe were under the bottom of the river. To install the well-tip, we had to dig a hole at the edge of the water, which is really hard to do without machinery. The hole fills up with water, and the sides collapse in. It was very slow work. My brother helped me dig with shovels until the hole was too deep to work without holding your breath, and I finished up, probably only getting another foot down.

I was laying on the ground on a some type of mat, head first, half in and half out of the hole, filling a spaghetti colander with rocks, while holding my breath underwater. My father was next to the hole, watching me fill the colander. When he saw me wave, he motioned to my brother, who was holding my feet, to slide me out of the hole with the colander. I'd dump the rocks, catch my breath, the water would clear up, and I'd go down again. I did get algae in my hair. The mat was surprisingly effective at keeping that side of the hole intact even though I was working there. I don't remember what the mat was made of and neither does my brother. I don't know how wide the hole was, but it was more cone than cup shaped and sometimes I would knock into the sides while getting rocks out of the bottom and the hole would partially fill itself in. That was maddening. Soon we decided it couldn't get deeper without getting a lot larger. So we went with that.

We got a big piece of re-bar and stuck it in the hole and hammered it down a bit so we could spin it around to loosen the rocks in the bottom of the hole. Then we worked the well tip into the loose rocks. I went underwater again to pull rocks up while they pushed the tip down, to try to get the tip further underground. I was pretty tired, so after that I got to hold the well tip upright while they slowly poured washed sand in the hole around the the mesh in the well-tip. We connected a capped, three foot pipe to the 90° elbow on the well tip, and put back the rocks, and it was completely underground, the tip about five and a half feet down. The elbow and pipe about a foot down.

This project was complicated by the efforts we took to protect the environment. We worked at the very edge of the water and created a rock dam around our project. We had one break in the downstream side of the wall that was one and a half inches wide and another in the upstream side to let clean water in. When I slowly removed a shovel full of rock and sand, dirty water would rise with the shovel, and our goal was to keep that stream of dirty water re-entering the river so small, it would not disturb any river residents. We piled the rock/sand mix we dug up about three feet away, on totally dry land. Just far enough away not to fall back into the hole until we needed it. We worked in slow motion, each shovel and hand full of rock was moved slowly so as not to overwhelm the rock wall with dirty water.

The next day, we attached new, 1½ inch galvanized pipe from the capped pipe to the pump. The water we pulled from that tip was the cleanest, purest water you can imagine. It made the best coffee and tea. Better than anything we'd ever had from a bottle or any other source, ever. Everyone who visited us commented on it. We miss that water!

But we still couldn't upgrade to a stronger, faster pump, unless we added more well tips, and I really didn't want to do that. The upside was that the ¾ hp pump could be run from our generator when the power was out, as it often was. And the gravity-fed water from the tank runs without power. Some folks on the river have wells that go down 30 feet or so, and they have a pump and pressure tank, so they need power to run more than a few gallons of water. We could fill up our new 1500 gallon tank and be good for more than a week without power. During winter rainy season, we always tried to get the tank filled just before rain started, because even though the water was filtered by the river bottom, when water is rising and very brown, the water we pumped was not totally clear. We couldn't see anything floating in it, but it was not perfectly clear, either. So there were still times where I would wait a long while between washing white laundry.

River Bottom Changes

Unfortunately, having a pipe in the bottom of the river is not a done deal. The river bottom changes every year. The river banks change, too. Every year, the rocks move a little further along their intended path to the ocean. When the river is really flowing fast from a hard storm you can hear the huge rocks hitting against each other as they are tumbled along the bottom of the river by the force of the water. Hearing those rocks hit each other can make you really understand why it's dangerous to fall into a raging river. Be afraid, those rocks will kill you. We were able to stand on our bridge in the middle of the river to hear those rocks moving. I didn't hear that sound from the bank of the river, though, so it didn't seem as dangerous from the riverbank.

It meant that our well tip could also change position and/or move downstream, but much to our delight, it stayed upright, and if it moved downstream, we couldn't tell. When I think about the different years of storms and excessive rain, I still can't believe it, my father was right. Well, not totally right. It rained so hard the pipe leading to the tip was broken away multiple times, and the tip was buried. Sometimes we couldn't find it and had to improvise. Then we went back to our original design of flexible pipe with a foot valve and floating bottle. And then, a season or two later, the river bottom changed again and the well-tip reappeared and we re-connected as if nothing ever happened.

Actually, a lot happened. The river banks change quite a bit over the years. It all depends on river flow and how much water is in the river at one time. High water is always powerful, expanding-the-width-of-the-river powerful. How that plays out as the water moves around the bend upstream is what determines how close the river was to our house and driveway.

Some years we had a lot of ground between us and the water and other years we didn't. If we had a lot of ground, it filled up within weeks with blackberry that grew tall; I was able to clear out areas for chairs to birdwatch from, and be hidden from the wildlife using the water. That was the best way to watch river life. If we lost riverbank, we had to watch from higher ground, right behind our house.

That was great the first eight years because a giant tanoak grew there, hiding us from the river and it's occupants. When that tree came down, it made such a change in the view, our whole sense of the river changed. It was suddenly a widescreen view with total clarity. From inside our house we could see so much, and even more from the bench outside. But we could also be seen by animals and people when we were on the bench. Not ideal.

In 1995, the year the river built the rock wall, three feet of sand had been deposited on the opposite bank, on top of the rocky, level bank we had when we installed the well tip and pipe. The force also disconnected the pipe from the tip. We wanted to get the pipe back on that rocky level, below the deposited sand, so it had a smaller chance of being ripped out again. To reconnect, we had to dig a trench through the sand, which got deeper the closer we got to the pump. Hard work. Rick and I took turns digging, but he took longer turns.

During our last few years in Big Sur, there were two big storms, one that washed away the deposited sand and exposed the pipe, and the second storm broke the pipe. Each of the storms dropped 10 inches of rain in 24 hours, record breaking storms. On a section further downstream from the well-tip, sand that had been deposited in 1995 was washed away in 2010, exposing some bricks that were still in the same odd position they were in when we last saw them 15 years before. I found it comforting. Here on the riverbank, with trees that are 1000 years old on each side of the river, things don't change all that quickly.

Basin Fire Side Effects

The Basin Fire, which burned through so much of Big Sur in 2008, didn't reach our house, thanks to the firemen! But it was a problem for many locals who lost their homes. Compared to the number of homes that burn in today's fires, like the Camp fire, it seems small, but it was overwhelming for those involved. For us, being evacuated was traumatic, wondering all day, every day, for weeks, if our house was still there, if our trees were still there. If they burn, the whole environment could change, mudslides may change the flow of the river, which controls our property line. One side of our property, the longest edge, ran down the middle of the river, where ever that may be. I had vivid dreams about waking up to look out the window and seeing all brown mud, everywhere, with redwood trunks all askew.

We were very lucky it was only a problem for our water system, and we didn't have any mudslides to outwit. After a big fire like that, what gets washed into the river is a lot of ash, mud and burned pieces of wood. The river water was too dirty to pull clear water from the surface for three years after the fire. The water was too heavy with sand and mud. You can't pump that, it ruins everything, and you can't use it anyway.

Before we were evacuated, we could see the ridge to the east from our house, and we watched the incredibly talented and *Oh My God Brave* bulldozer driver, risking his life to carve a firebreak at the tippy top of the ridge, all to save our lives, homes and the redwoods. We were in our house cheering him on, gob-smacked that he was up there, working. We really didn't want to distract him or we'd have gone outside to cheer him. But man, he did a great job! Hero doesn't seem a big enough word to describe him. My understanding is the bulldozer driver was a Volunteer Fireman. A volunteer!

We were lucky to have time to pack for our evacuation, had time to take one long last look, in case it wasn't the same when we returned. We spent weeks at my sister's house, and we returned to find lots of burned areas on the east side of Highway One. We didn't see burns on the west side at all. The areas where houses burned and other areas that burned too hot to regenerate were not easily visible from Highway One, and the burned areas we saw were able to regenerate themselves quickly. A drive along the coast was still utterly beautiful.

I went to local meetings about what was being done to help recover the area and keep mudslides from forming. Hearing about the mudslides that might come our way was scary. Considering the places that might become a problem, we wondered where we could park our car out of the way. Turns out there was nowhere nearby that could be deemed safe for our car that we could also get to safely from our house. It seemed possible the river could get blocked by a mudslide and we'd be spending the winter in a tent on the hill. The very nightmare my sister imagined.

After the fire, we were again grateful as we watched contractors install K-rail concrete barriers on the road to the ridge, in an effort to guide a possible mud flow away from the highway. It was a brilliant white banner of concern. The area had been backburned on the east side of Highway One for a long distance to get control of the fire and keep it out of the Big Sur Valley. It worked! Many, many thanks to the firemen!

What the fire meant to me that year was, I had to find our well-tip and connect to it so we could draw water that was filtered by the river bottom itself. We had a 4,995 gal. water tank delivered to the Back Point Forty, just in case the water we pumped wasn't clean enough, we'd at least have that to ration. That's the biggest tank you can have without a permit. They're everywhere.

I connected the new tank to our 1500 gal. tank by adding a T-connector with an on/off valve at the in-line to the small tank. Rick ran

50 feet of pipe from there to the big tank, and I installed the connections at that end, and an on/off hose valve there, too. We could have filled it right away with the surface water we had been drawing for two years, but we didn't fill the tank right away. I wanted to wait till it was closer to rain, to pump just before rain, so it would be as fresh as possible. But we were able to fill the big tank with the same little shallow well jet pump we used to fill the 1500 gal. tank, getting it to pump twice as high as the specs called for.

I wasn't sure anything would work once rain started, though, and for back up I asked a well driller for an estimate. He wanted $30,000 for a 30 foot deep well. Plus whatever it would cost to connect that to the house. After he left, I went on an immediate and diligent search and found our well tip. We connected it to our pump again and got clean water right away. We filled the big tank with that water, but we still weren't sure the water would pump clear after rain started. If we needed to use the water in the big tank, I would have had to add another pump to get water from the big tank to the smaller tank.

The first rain after the fire was shocking. The river water was so dark, it was like dark chocolate syrup, thick, with slow waves. As soon as the rain stopped, we ran the pump, and got pretty clean water, not perfectly clear, but cleaner than the water we usually drew from the surface during the winter. And still the best coffee and tea you can imagine.

But there was one comical thing that happened every year on the riverbank. Without fail, I found at least one pair of men's underwear had washed downstream and become entangled in the plant life on the bank near our house. Every year.

Property Management

Having lived in the suburbs in a rented house, I was no expert in property management. But here I was with the responsibility of not ruining the place, or killing anything. I had a lot to learn. I bought a lot of books and read up on the trees and the environment. I read about the wildflowers, and tried to find info on the birds and bugs we saw.

Other than some redwoods leaning precariously toward the house, everything seemed healthy to me, except for what looked like fire blight on the branch tips of every tanoak sapling on the property. I read up on fire blight and asked at the nurseries what could be done, and the answer was astonishing. There was nothing I could do. You can't really treat the forest without affecting an enormous amount of other species, none of which need to be treated.

And then there's the question of how it could be done. I'd need a fire truck, or an airplane. It's just not practical to try to treat even small areas of a forest. And according to the books, the blight would go away on it's own over time, so I put fire blight in the back of my mind to think about more pressing things. It never went away.

Our little two acres had such dense stands of tanoak, and along with the young saplings that had the fire blight, the older, 100 foot tall tanoaks all had numerous, unsightly (to me, anyway) charcoal-like half-spheres attached to their trunks. I never did find out exactly what that was. It was on every mature tanoak there.

I was not thrilled with the tanoaks. Next to the redwoods, the tanoaks were ugly and distracted from the view. But there was one nice, healthy, young tree, about 35 feet tall that was in perfect condition. It was in the *Back Point Forty* and we saw it twice a day when we went for our daily walks around the place, you know, to check things out. This tree was really beautiful, and it changed my mind about tanoaks in general. I started to appreciate them, to see their beauty, and see their acorns for the resources they were to the animals, and I hoped this fire blight would go away, so I could enjoy the dense stands of saplings. But it wasn't fire blight after all, it was Sudden Oak Death (SOD), it's just that no one knew it yet.

One day my young beautiful tree turned completely brown, every leaf, top to bottom, all brown, overnight. And the leaves hung on the tree. None of them fell off like dead leaves usually do. My beautiful tree had died suddenly, and I wanted some answers. None of my books covered anything like that. It was 1995, and I started looking for information in the news that might tell me what was going on.

I wasn't yet familiar with the California university system's master gardener programs, so I didn't know I could have called them, but somewhere around 1997, I read a big story in the Monterey paper that talked about how SOD had been discovered in Big Sur in 96. Apparently, a neighbor nearby had called the local master garden specialist to come look at their tree that had turned brown and died overnight, too. It became a big thing.

As time went on, I could see that there were signs on every tanoak in our neck of the woods, which was about 10 acres around our house. All the trees had sections of dead, brown leaves that hung on the tree, sections that grew larger over time. Every one. So we had to face the fact that our woods were changing, and we were about to loose more than a third of all the trees we could see. That is so many trees, there is no way to count them. Our first response was to stop walking around so much because it was clearly dangerous. Branches were falling off trees, tanoaks and oak trees were falling over all around us, something came down almost every day.

One dark night we heard a crashing outside that was so loud, we ran to the back door to get out of the house. We were so sure a tree was going to get us. It sounded like it was coming right through the front door. But the tree hit the ground before we got out, and with so much force it shook the whole house like an earthquake. We were surprised the tree didn't break our front sliding doors, it seemed so close.

We went to the front door and opened it to a swirling mass of dust and leaves and flying dirt. There was so much stuff blowing around, I wouldn't have been surprised to see Dorothy and Toto fly by; we slammed the door closed and opened the shades to see what we could, and it took quite a while for the dust to fall from the air. And when we opened the door again to shine flashlights around, we couldn't see any fallen trees at all.

The next morning, we went out to search and found the tree top was about 100 feet from our front door, and it's base was another 100 feet beyond that. It wasn't even our tree. And we were really shocked to see which tree had fallen, because it didn't seem dead, it wasn't brown all over, just in a few small spots. It had been one of the seriously giant tanoaks, about 3½ feet diameter, with giant branches, and it had taken a lot of other tree's branches with it when it fell.

It fell because it had a hidden giant hole inside it's base that was caused by regular old root rot; we had no idea it was so stressed and likely to fall. The bark looked pretty normal. The tree left a huge mess. Considering how far from the house it fell, we were taken aback by the dirt flying through the air at our front door. Everything around us was covered with that dust and dirt. Everything. We left the tree alone, except to walk on the trunk as a new path through the woods.

There were a few more articles in the paper about SOD and I think it was after 2000 that I read a new article that said what property owners should do to reduce the spread of it. I took it as homeowner instructions that should be followed by everyone, so I did what the good folks at Berkley said to do.

I was grateful, finally, for some actual advice, we were afraid of having a branch, or worse, a tree, fall on a guest. We also became more aware of the fire hazard increasing all around us. We had to get rid of this fire fuel, there was so much dead tanoak around us, we were afraid a small spark could ignite the whole place and the fire would burn so hot, it might take down the old growth redwoods all around us. With dead tanoaks all over the hillside, up to the ridge, fire would follow the dead trees right up the ridge to the many homes there. We may as well have been living on top of kindling.

The instructions from Berkley told us to cut down the dead and dying trees and burn them, including the brush. I hired a local guy to start the job. Kelly had a great crew of local guys, they had an incredible work ethic, and were easy to get along with as well. I found them in the local newspaper, the RoundUp, which is the same local paper they've had in Big Sur for 69 years.

When I was reading it, it was printed out on legal sized paper, but it had been mimeographed before that. Maybe it's only on Facebook now. Anyone in town could place an ad in The RoundUp, it was free. And any local could send in articles or notices that the whole town needed to see. The volunteers who published it knew everybody in Big Sur, so it was easy for them to keep it local. It was lovely, and so personal. I looked forward to it every month.

The crew came by, it seemed like every other week, to remove another tanoak. Some of these trees were big, 2+ feet in diameter, and many were leaning in scary ways. We felt unsafe in our own yard. Later, Kelly worked on a research team studying SOD and became quite knowledgeable. According to suddenoakdeath.org, "*Phytophthora ramorum* is a plant pathogen that causes Sudden Oak Death (SOD) as well as a foliar/twig disease (Ramorum blight) in other susceptible plants." So it was probably ramorum blight on the saplings, not fire blight.

This crew cut down all the giant dying tanoaks around our buildings, over 5 years time. And what that meant to our property was an intense need for fire clearance. Suddenly we had enough sunlight hitting the ground that things started to grow with a vengeance. It doesn't take very much sun to grow poison oak, blackberry, and bracken fern. Seems these things grow with abandon from just being shown a picture of the sun.

These are woody plants that must be removed to the ground for true fire clearance, and they're not happy about it, so they fight back. Bracken fern stems will slice through your gloves to get to your skin. Whatever cutting tool you use, bracken fern leaves a sharp edge, and don't even think you can bend the stem to break it and walk away with the fern. Oh no, it will not let go, ever, unless you have a tool sharp enough to cut the stem, which, of course, leaves a sharpened stem, so you can never win. The sharp stems are terrible for little dogs and wild animals. I don't know why rope isn't made from bracken fern. To remove it you have to dig down with a very sharp blade to cut through the roots. And make sure to get all the roots out, or it will be back in a jiffy. Maybe it should be called Jiffy Fern.

Blackberry has an abundance of thorns, and like poison oak, will surprise you with spring-traps of branches swirling around to smack you in the face while you work. It's so fun!

We weren't really sure the poison oak was poison oak at first because it wasn't like the poison oak we knew. We were familiar with poison oak that was small leaved, very shiny, with the leaves almost curled under, dark green and tinged with red. It climbed up things to get more sun. It was obvious. This stuff that grew in the shade was like a delicate shade plant. The leaves were flat and low gloss, a pale green, they grew on woody stems in piles, with stems that grew long and rather spindly, with not that many leaves. We saw it growing by the driveway, and as we walked past, we could see the under side of the plant, and there were tiny, delicate, charming, whitish-greenish flower clumps under there being pollinated by bumble bees. Dark purple berries came in the fall, and the birds love those things. I guess birds think they can never have enough poison oak berries, so they spread it around as best they can.

We didn't have enough sun, even after the tanoaks were gone, for the blackberry bushes to make ripe, tasty blackberries, though. We were in a very steep valley, and had reduced sunlight hours from most people in Big Sur. We tried every year to find some sweet berries, but I think over the entire 21 years, we probably only had 100 at the very most. The bushes grow like crazy, but the berries just don't sweeten up. I tried many times to grow tomatoes, too, but never got more than 3 tomatoes, even on a very well developed plant, and they didn't ripen enough.

The fire-clearance conundrum is that when you take plants down to the ground, you're left with bare dirt. Bare dirt that attracts thousands more weed and tree seeds than you've ever seen before. Seems within minutes, the ground is covered with 6 inch tall plants that threaten to take over, and if you don't get rid of them quickly, there will be 10 times more work to do next week. Well, I may be exaggerating, but just a little.

If you can manage to keep the plants down to the ground, you're left with the bare-earth, outside-to-inside transference, where more and more of the outside dirt comes in the house with you. No matter how good your door mat is, it will not keep dirt out of your house if your paths are dirt. So, what to do?

For many years I kept a thick layer of redwood chips on the major path from the bridge to the house. Redwood chips are one of the many natural resources that came with a wooded property, that I miss. With redwoods, there is always a small tree that needs to be removed and chipped up, much to my surprise. They grow like weeds. Not so much from seed, but from sucker growth.

If the tippy top of a redwood is damaged in any way, it sends a message to the bazillion growth buds at the base to start growing, and they never stop. Every year the suckers need to be cut back. If you don't, they are in a competition to see which sucker can grow the biggest the fastest, and become too large to remove, while they steal nutrition from the parent tree. So you have to keep up. I don't know at what age the growth buds stop making new suckers, but all the redwoods on our property had suckers growing at the base, except for Old Tom. He had no suckers at the bottom, even though he had damage at the top. I took to trimming the suckers with a hedge trimmer.

There was a row of small redwoods growing along the bank of the river by the driveway, and when we moved in, I planned to sort of farm them, cutting each down just before it was 12 inches in diameter, the point at which you must have a permit to remove them. Then I let one of it's suckers grow to replace it. I could use the trunk to make edging for the gardens, in either large long pieces or as short pieces standing upright, next to each other. I've done both. Whatever is left is chipped up for using on paths or as mulch in the gardens. There is no better material in the world for garden mulch than redwood chips. Lasts for years, breaks down to become more beautiful soil.

We couldn't get redwood bark chips though. Stripping bark from big redwoods is hard work, and only done on trees that have been cut down. The little things we cut down in the course of fire clearance didn't have well enough developed bark to be useful that way, and we never stripped the small logs of bark. So I didn't use bark chips. But I quit trying to farm those trees when SOD took over, we needed all the trees we could get along the river bank, to keep the bank the bank.

There had been a fire through the area in the early 1900's, and we could see the evidence of this fire all around us, really. Almost every large redwood on the northeast side of our property had some burn damage, large damage. On the redwoods that make up what became the wedding ring, on the northwest sides, the bark has been burned, and it's black, black, black. But on the other sides, it's just fine. We could see how the redwoods grew from keeping an eye on that burned bark. The crevices in the burned bark split apart from new growth, so we could see the start of fresh new redwood colored bark, growing in about one inch wide vertical stripes between the black, burned bark, as the trees grew and the trunks got wider. That means it took more than 75 years for those burned redwoods to recover just that much. These trees hadn't been killed by the fire, but lost many branches.

Fire can damage trees at their base in a different way. Trees that are near hills have the added risk in fire of a burning log rolling down a hill and getting stopped by a tree. The log lying on the ground will burn for a long time up against the base of a standing tree, and it burns a hole in the base. If it's a large log burning, it will leave a large hole in the base of the trunk, maybe large enough to make the tree fall over from fire. There was a tree like that we called the Pivot Point, in the woods just off our property.

Redwoods are supposed to grow straight from the ground, with no taper to the trunk. This tree had had a big taper at the base, which was completely hollowed out by the fire. The stump was nearly 15 feet tall at it's tallest point. It was really just a shell of the stump, large enough a group of six people could gather inside it. It appeared the fire was really big and swirled around like a tornado inside the base of the tree. The entire tree stump was black inside with charcoal, and the bark outside was in a swirling pattern, which is why we called it the Pivot Point. It looked like the tree itself was lying on the ground right next to the stump, and it was about four feet diameter. Trees as large as this rot slowly on the ground, taking maybe 500 years to become dirt It looked to me like this tree may have been on the ground for about half that long. We would take our guests to the Pivot Point on our walks, stand inside the stump to marvel at it, then climb up onto it's downed trunk to use as a 100 foot long path, to get to another point on the river.

Walking along this tree made clear the difference between an old growth tree and a young, 100 or 200 year old tree. It's the branches. A young tree will have branches that are long, but thin, three, four, or five inches in diameter at their largest point. An old growth tree's branches are different. They're mature trees in themselves. The branches on Old Tom are 14 inches in diameter and larger, with large branches, nearly the same size, growing on them.

Now I look at the branches, see how thick they are, and look at the width of the tree, not all old growth trees are enormous at the base, some are merely giants. But they often have compression at the base just from the weight of the tree itself compressing the fibers of the wood. This compression makes the bark gnarly, not all vertical crevices, but angled and out of alignment.

There is an old growth tree near our neighbor's house that has, at the very top, one old growth branch. I guess over the years, all the other branches have been blown off and replaced by younger branches. This branch is twice as long and thick as all the others on the tree and looks conspicuous. So I added checking the trunk for signs of larger, broken off branches to my personal checklist for old growth. Before I understood that it was an old growth branch, every time I looked at it I imagined cutting that branch off to make it even with the other branches. As I became more aware of the environment, though, I valued it more. It was an example I could point out to others. Everyone who came to the house wanted to know how to tell if a redwood was old growth.

On a younger redwood tree, the smaller three, four, or five inch diameter branches can tear off in a high wind of 45 mph or more. A neighbor had a branch fall on, or through, the skylight over his bed in a 77 mph wind. That branch was big, more like six inches diameter and he said he was lucky he wasn't in bed at the time, or he'd have been killed. He was unable to remove the branch without totally destroying the skylight, so he patched it up with silicone caulk, and cut the branch off above and below the skylight. Worked great. It was quite a sight, and a reminder of how fragile life is. Talk about a conversation starter. That's what they mean by "widow maker."

We could see a giant redwood in the Back Point Forty leaning on another redwood, threatening to take them both down sometime soon. Fortunately, if they fell, they would fall away from our house and paths. During high wind, those trees would groan like ghosts as they swayed in the wind, rubbing against each other. Like the forest was making a running commentary on the wind, just for us. It didn't take a really high wind to get them talking, either, just 25 mph.

Within a few years we found ourselves in the terrible position of having to remove a redwood, one that was about six feet away from our house. It was between the house and the water tank. The tree had a problem, a hole in the base burned by fire. An undesirable situation.

A redwood tree with a hole in the base is a danger and will fall over at some point, probably before it's time. When, is the question, and how long can it support it's own weight before it falls? 100 years? It had already been 75. How big is that hole? How heavy is the growth on the tree? How much is it leaning? Where is it likely to fall and how many other trees will it take with it if it falls? As a forest manager and homeowner, there is a lot to consider.

Unfortunately, we had to consider the sucker that was growing from inside the burn hole in the base of the redwood. This sucker seemed to grow overnight and was suddenly more than a foot in diameter, which meant I wasn't allowed to cut it down. Anything larger than 12 inches had to have county approval to remove.

The thing is, the big tree with the hole in the base was a danger to the house and us inside, even if it didn't have a sucker growing inside it. It had a compromised base that could not fully support the weight of the growth at the top, which was going to town. It would come down eventually, whereas the young sucker growing from inside the hole was really healthy, and obviously growing fast.

If the sucker grew much more, it would push the big tree over, right on to the house. Besides destroying our house, it would probably damage the redwoods at the other end of our house. Then the sucker would get the prime growth spot, and be healthier for the long run. And it's not like that would kill the big tree, the sucker was growing from the same roots as the big tree. My understanding is once the big tree is gone, the sucker tree gets all the nourishment from the roots of both trees, so it can grow really fast and will be almost as big around as the tree it replaced in just 50 years or so. The original tree took nearly 300 years to grow that large.

But this second growth tree will not have the strong, tiny wood grain of the original. It's a different animal, and wood milled from it can't support the weight an old growth board can support.

Well, that's how it was explained to me by the Arborist who wrote the report and the county, who gave us a waiver (permission) to remove the big tree and keep the sucker. We hired a Tree Surgeon, Quinn, from south Big Sur to help us out. He had a reputation for doing the best big tree work around. He gave us an incredible price because he said he could lumberjack the tree and use the wood himself. Lumber-jacking meant he would cut the tree at it's base and let it fall. First, he had to climb the tree and remove the branches as he went, lowering them to the ground with pulleys and rope. He cut the very top off and lowered it, too. The top and all the branches were chipped up by his crew.

He tied a very long rope to the top of the tree. He planned to fell the tree so it landed between two similar trees that had space enough between them. The tree would fall crosswise over another old, down redwood, about 100 feet away, that he expected it would crack over, distributing the weight of the fall further throughout the woods. He climbed one of the redwoods the tree would fall between to put the long rope up over a very sturdy branch. He parked his truck off to the side just a little further away, and tied the rope to the truck. Then he started to cut the tree at the base. He cut a wedge in the side he wanted the tree to fall on, then sliced through the tree with a very big chainsaw, almost completely through. As he went, he hammered "wedges" into the cut the chainsaw was making to the keep the weight of the tree from closing the space up. Wedges are surprisingly small considering their importance. Maybe six inches long and one inch at the wide end. If the cut gets closed up, the chainsaw will get stuck in the tree and can't be removed.

All this took some time. He was a very powerful guy with a very powerful chainsaw, and it was a pleasure to watch an expert work. He left a small section uncut, to keep the trunk lined up while he finished getting it ready to fall. He chained the trunk to itself above and below the cut, to keep the base from rolling down hill and knocking over the house. Then he got in the truck and moved it forward ever so slightly, pulling at the top of the redwood.

The tree fell exactly where he planned, and cracked right where he thought it would. And that piece he didn't cut through broke off, flew up in the air, and landed on a metal table making a very loud, finishing gong. Much as we hated to lose a redwood, we had been living in fear of that tree falling for a while.

Quinn, the Tree Surgeon, came back a few days later to cut the trunk away from the fire road it crossed. Fire roads are made so a fire truck can get in and out in emergencies. Our fire road started at the top of the highway, and was, in fact, our driveway, from the highway, across the meadow, across the river, across our property and green space to our nearest neighbor's house. That particular road stopped there.

But it was our responsibility to keep that road clear and passable, in case there was a fire at our, or our neighbor's house. A fire road is 14 feet wide, and must be kept completely clear, so a fire truck could come by anytime they needed to. I took that responsibility seriously. And as a volunteer fireman, Quinn did, too, so he came back to open that section up.

He sliced through that trunk with such ease, he could have been cutting butter. He cut sections of "rounds," each one about a 10 inch thick slice of trunk. And they were perfectly flat, straight cuts, like I could use them to tile a floor. And that got me thinking about how I could use those rounds. A stage for the bride and groom, maybe? Quinn had done the job in trade for the wood. But after he cut it down, he found he couldn't use it after all, it had too much water rot.

People can get a romanticized vision of redwood trees, where they see them as indestructible. I know I did, that's partly why we were in Big Sur. But it's not true, redwoods can be damaged by too much water, and you can see the damage in the wood when it's milled or cut. Quinn pointed out the holes in the wood made by excess water, and pointed to the rain gutter of our house that dumped water right on the ground next to the tree trunk. We could all see the tree wasn't going to be worth the trouble to mill up. After this, we put up different gutters, and I attached 20 feet of accordion gutter extension to the new downspouts to get the water as far away from the house and trees as I could

This romanticized vision of indestructible redwoods leads people to place their homes inappropriately close to redwoods, like ours was. Fortunately, the last I heard, the closest you could build to a large redwood in Monterey County was 12 feet. Maybe that's far enough. Time will tell.

Anyway, we paid Quinn to cut the rest up in rounds that I decided to use in what became the redwood wedding ring, to make a floor inside the ring for weddings.

I had been working to get the grounds readied to be able to have small weddings on our property, and I found a very special place to do that. I didn't realize it when we first moved in, but the old growth redwood tree that was holding up our bridge was one of many in a ring of redwoods that measured 16x32 feet on the inside of the ring. Large enough to have really beautiful weddings there. And there is symbolism in crossing a foot bridge to get married in a ring made of trees, some of which are 800 and 1000 years old.

We hired Bill, a mason, to lay the floor, as Quinn cut the rounds. Quinn was nervous this time about getting each round the same size. He had measuring equipment all around, but told me he didn't think he could get them all perfect. I told him to forget making them perfect, to just cut the way he did on the fire road. He did, and those cuts were closer to perfect than the ones he tried to measure. Bill did a beautiful job, too, and the floor looked stunning. I wished I could get married there.

A few years later, Quinn's team came through and transformed our property with a week of fire clearance work. But we had some miscommunication. I had pointed to three specific trees on our property I wanted taken down. The trees I wanted taken down were the only ones I thought I could legally remove, as all the other dead tanoaks behind them were not on our property. What *they saw* was me sweeping my pointed finger across the whole field of them, from one side to the other. So they thought I had asked for the entire field of dead tanoaks to be removed. Fortunately, they removed the whole fire danger. Unfortunately, it was not our property.

I don't remember what we were working on inside the house that week, but I was really busy, trusted them, and didn't want to get in their way. So I was pretty stunned when I looked outside and saw the whole field of dead trees cut down. I told them what I had really asked for, and we were all chagrined. They were volunteer fireman, and said, "Well, it all had to go, it was a real danger." We absolutely agreed, and were happy about it, except for the cost.

The firemen didn't just cut down the trees though, they really cleaned up the place, which left a nearly flat sandy field in it's place. This field was more than 100 feet by 75 feet. They removed all the tree stumps from the area and they made a big brush pile where they burned it all up. We were assured by the Berkley folks (I emailed them) that burning was the right thing to do.

Just 3 years later the Basin Complex Fire, a massive wildfire in Big Sur, started on June 21, 2008, the result of a lightning strike. We were evacuated, and watched the ridge across the highway from our place going up in flames, on TV news, from my sister's place in the Bay Area. We thought if they hadn't cut those trees down, the falling/blowing embers would have ignited that field, and the whole Big Sur valley could have gone up in flames from there. There was so much dead tanoak there.

I spread flower seeds all over the bare ground, on what we now called the "meadow," just in time for rain. It was delightful. Unfortunately, the flower seeds I bought were labeled as California Native seeds, and they were not. So we had foxglove and sweet william and sweet pea, flowers I love, but would never have purposely planted in a natural meadow. Soon bracken fern took over quite a bit of the meadow, too. That fern is native to the world.

Just after the tree guys left the property, a professor from Berkley stopped by to check out the SOD issues we had. He smiled broadly at the bare ground and said we had absolutely done the right thing for our property. That was reassuring. But when I asked what we could replant the area with to return it to woods, he said not to plant anything native. It would just die again. A depressing thing for a native plant lover to hear.

No one else in Big Sur was able to remove so much dead tanoak so quickly, because Monterey County seemed to believe that dead trees were healthy for forests, and should be left to decay naturally. Homeowners in Big Sur were freaking out about it. They wanted to get rid of their dead trees to stop further spread, and because of the fire danger, besides, dead trees are ugly and dangerous, they always fall down.

The county should have given us all permission to do what needed to be done, everyone knew what the problem was by then. Because we were isolated from our neighbor's view, we were able to remove it all without anyone stopping us. We were told by the firemen that because the owner of the dead oaks had abandoned that piece of property, never coming by to keep an eye on it, we were allowed to care-take the trees for the health of our own property. I didn't know how true that was but it sounded good to me.

Researchers discovered SOD was a new mutation of standard old root rot, a fungus we knew was also all around us, and we wondered what would make that happen. I thought about Methyl tert-butyl ether (MTBE), a gasoline additive used as an oxygenate and to raise the octane number of gasoline. It was in use in both California and Germany at the time, and both places were considered ground zero for SOD.

But there was one great thing to come out of SOD. The winter wren's favorite environment of piles of brush was multiplied many times over by each naturally falling tree, so their population grew and we got to hear their beautiful songs all around us. They are a very small, uncommon bird of forests, just 3½ inches beak to tail. and dressed in a sort of brown pinstriped suit. Very smart dresser! They have the shortest tail of all the wrens, and they hold it straight up in the normal wren-like fashion. And they bob up and down a lot, as if they are tiny American dippers, but with a much more complicated song, a master musician. I count myself lucky to have ever seen or heard a winter wren. As he sings, he moves his head up and down and side to side, which throws his voice very far and wide, adding volume-control quality to the tune. And the bird is so tiny! One of the delights of nature is that a being that small can make a sound that big. That loud. It can sound like he's singing on my shoulder, but I'm watching him sing 75 feet up a tree.

As the winter wrens population exploded, the acorn woodpecker's and the Stellar's jay's population shrank. The number of acorns to feed them had drastically fallen to less than a quarter of their normal supply, so we heard less and less of their raucous calls and arguments. As the trees fell, their roosting holes fell with them, further and further reducing the available useful environment for the acorn woodpeckers and the Stellar's jays, who steal the woodpecker's nest holes. And that left a quiet that was filled by the song of the winter wren. But the falling tanoaks caused other problems as well.

One year our power went out when one of our power lines was snagged by a falling tanoak. We couldn't see the end of the wire, which meant it was probably hanging in the woods on the other side of the river. Rick went over with a fire extinguisher to see what was going on, and I called PG&E. They asked for him to wait there till PG&E arrived on site, which was more than an hour.

Meanwhile, I had called the Big Sur Volunteer Fire Brigade, and they came out to help. There was fire burning up in the trees when Rick got there, and he was able to put that out with the fire extinguisher, but it was empty when a small fire developed on the ground around the end of the down wire. The volunteer fireman arrived just in time and buried it with scoops from a large scoop shovel.

It was an eye-opener for us. We had to be more proactive against fire. These first responders can't be there right away, and everywhere you are in Big Sur is very far from anyone who can help you. We got bunches of shovels and fire-clearance tools and I got to work outside doing more fire clearance. Rick had to be in the house, in the office, so I got to do, or manage, the outside work, and I loved it.

My father wanted to help me do it, too, even from New Jersey. He attached a winch to the front of our big truck, because he knew a lot about living in the country. He knew we'd need it, and we really did. The first thing we did with it was to pull our new 1500 gallon water tank up the hill to replace the wine vat. Brian,* our beloved horn playing contractor, who had worked for us through multiple projects, made a sled for the tank, and we pulled it up hill with the winch cable through a fixed pulley, which was attached to a live oak growing above the water tank.

I'm not sure how Brian did it, but he made the plywood curve up on the leading edge of the sled, so very few of the plants the sled slid over were damaged in the process.

He had already removed the wine vat, and replaced the plywood the vat had been sitting on. He attached new, very thick plywood to the original concrete blocks with an explosive, nail shooting gun. Loved that. Then he and Rick guided the tank into position while I worked the winch. When it was in the right place, I connected new plumbing pipes to the new tank, and had that puppy filled before dark. A really great, fun day!

We used the winch to move a lot of logs, there were so many on the ground, all around us. It was part of the fire clearance work we needed. A few years after that, the oak tree over the water tank died, and we needed to get it down before it fell on and damaged our water tank. But it was in such a precarious position on the hill, there was no place to stand to cut it down. Rick and Brian came up with a plan, one I was sure would get them on the Internet. Rick perched above the oak, with the chainsaw, draping himself over the stump of an ancient Laurel, so he could reach the trunk of the oak. Brian, with a 100 pounds on Rick, stood behind him and held on to his belt, allowing Rick to reach far enough down the hill to cut the tree down. I could barely watch, but the tree came down, didn't hit the tank and no one was hurt!

Redwood Removal

Unfortunately, we had to remove another redwood, on the other side of our house. It was much closer to the house, only eight inches away. It had always leaned a bit more than many guests were comfortable with, but now it was getting worse. On the opposite side of the lean, the ground was lifting up around the base of the tree, a clear sign of trouble to come and roots breaking. But the Arborist we hired to examine the tree and write a report to the county, explaining the tree was a danger and in the process of falling, well, he somehow failed to mention that in his report. When our request for a waiver was denied, I had to contact both the county and the Arborist. We were so worried about the tree, we were contemplating moving to a hotel until we could have it removed.

The Arborist did nothing. I managed to contact the planning department and got an email address for the planner in charge of trees, where I sent pictures we took ourselves. I pointed out on the pictures both the lean of the tree and the ground lifting on the opposite side, and also pointed out the compression of the trunk at the base of the tree. I got a call from the planner, who asked to come by to see the tree the next day. She saw what I saw and got us the waiver. The waiver allowed us to remove the tree without paying a fee; if we wanted to remove a healthy tree, we would have to have a damn good reason and then pay a permit fee of thousands of dollars to get permission.

We wanted to do something special with the wood from this tree, we hoped it wasn't damaged by water. We hoped selling the wood would cover the cost of removing it. And it did, but it took time. We got a team together for the job. We knew some of these guys because they worked for us before, and they brought their friends who also did this kind of work. They were all strong, young guys who knew what they were doing and worked so hard. And everything worked out just fine.

We paid Donnie* and his cutting crew to get each section on the ground. He removed all the branches first, then cut mostly 12 foot sections off the tree, because that was all the room we had to work with there, in front of the house. This tree was pretty big, more than two feet diameter at the top, seven at the bottom. Donnie did the actual cutting, so many cuts, and wow, is he powerful! I have only used a chainsaw once, and I knew immediately that I should never, ever do that again. I'm not strong enough to handle it. But it made me really appreciate the risks these guys face. (Ever since then, every man holding a chainsaw looks more handsome to me:)

Then the miller cut each log into three and four inch thick slabs. This whole process was work intensive, and very loud. The chainsaws to cut the tree, and the saws to mill the wood are very big and have to be sharpened often. The milling was done in exchange for half the wood slabs. We were thrilled. We did manage to sell the slabs, and many were bought by Ventana Inn. I heard the slabs they used to make outdoor tables were burned in a fire that destroyed their kitchen. But the slab they bought for the reception desk was still in use when I was last there.

You can't live in the woods without hiring neighbors to help you out. People who live in the rural world have difficulty finding work, though, because the jobs available are often short term jobs that come and go. It's hard to support yourself even if you have a business that your neighbors need. They don't always need you. It might be easier in tourist environments, but there are so few purposeful long term jobs in the rural/tourist world. Many tourist businesses treat their workers terribly, and pay next to nothing. Folks buy property to work themselves, so they only need help part-time, and then they find they need jobs, too. But hard workers all, in my experience. I'm a hard worker myself, and these guys impressed the hell out of me.

We tried to hire folks we liked enough to be friends with, and that worked out for us. The guy who helped us get the second redwood milled up was an often charming character, a Korean War Vet, an older man who worked so hard I was shocked. He and his wife raised their children on the south coast of Big Sur, where he worked as a caretaker at the time. The spot was special, even among special spots, and it was a community meeting place, where locals had big parties to celebrate everything, and also funerals, to pay respects to those past. I went to one gathering there, a huge, beautiful party for the funeral of his ex-wife.

The spot was made for gatherings, with lots of shady as well as sunny areas. There was a large lawn at the top of a huge cliff over looking the blue, blue Pacific Ocean. There was a stage and multiple places for bands to set up. The house was very tiny, as most older houses in Big Sur are, and they used the house as mostly a kitchen. My understanding is the kids slept in other buildings and barns, and said goodnight to the brilliant stars, while falling asleep to the sound of the waves so close. Seemed like heaven to me.

I say "often charming" about this guy because we argued a lot. He'll stand up to anyone he thinks is wrong, and I admire that. He was a great story teller and knew so much about growing everything. He had a family of many sons who sometimes worked with him, good sons who worked hard, and at least one of whom was a volunteer firefighter with the Brigade. He and his family helped us prepare our property for sale about five years after the milling. And we really needed the help.

Some of the work he did to get the property ready involved removing a lot of stumps. All the tanoaks previously removed around our house left big stumps, and they were ugly and limited the usefulness of the property. He dug out around each one, down far enough that he could get a chainsaw under there and cut through the many large roots, and then pulled the stump out with his truck. Large flat areas were left for me to ready for grass seed.

When we moved in, we were thinking, yeah, no more mowing lawns! Like we thought the woods would be less work than mowing our little lawn in the Bay Area. Such idiots we were, really. We thought, it's a natural environment, how much work could be involved? Back breaking work is involved!! Raking leaves is nothing compared to raking duff off the path. That stuff is heavy, and we needed to have the path always cleared of duff so we could pull our wagons of groceries to the house. There is always work in the woods. Something is either growing out of control, or dying. Always, always work in the woods!

But when the stumps were cleared out, we had larger bare areas that would invite the whole host of plant thugs to take up residence if I didn't plant something there first. I looked around for ground covers that would be nice to live around, but when you make the comparisons, grass is inexpensive compared to other plants, reasonably easy to install and maintain, looks fabulous, and helps keep moisture in the ground by shading it. And so pretty. After not seeing a blade of grass for nearly 20 years, grass suddenly seemed so perfect.

So I read up on how to install a lawn, and bought seed. This changed the look of the place from woods to park, a beautiful lawn next to the river, perfect for weddings in the redwood wedding ring, right? It was commercial property, and when we put it on the market, we highlighted that aspect. If we had actually been having weddings there, we probably could have gotten more for the place, but Rick was working for a start up tech company at the time, and he didn't have the time to work with me to make weddings happen.

Part 2: Pictures

When we moved in, digital cameras were not available, and picture taking took some prep work, to be able to have a camera at the ready. We decided when we moved in that we would rather just live our lives there, and not try to document everything as it happened. I rarely, even now, take pictures, but Rick kept up with the technology enough to take some pictures worth sharing. Some are digital, some very old digital, some are even Polaroids that we scanned in.

A ground level view of the river, looking downstream, over the driveway. The rain has stopped and the river is just starting to recede. In this picture, the bottom right shows the water covering the driveway. The water is about 4 feet higher than it is in summer. During a really big storm, the water covers all the ground on the right, to the edge of the picture.

Looking downstream from the bridge. It's later in the year, the water is low enough to break up over the rocks.

The Back Point Forty, before Sudden Oak Death killed off the understory. It is so dense with tanoak, the fire road isn't visible.

This picture was taken from the fire road in the Back Point Forty, after most of the dead tanoak had been removed. We can see clear to the sun shed.

This is what Sudden Oak Death looks like, killing off the tanoak saplings. These saplings all appeared to have fire blight when we first saw them. This picture was taken in the back Point Forty. It was dreary like this for years.

The Pivot Point, with our little dog Teddy Bear. You can see the two sections are all that is left of the base of the redwood. We weren't sure, but it looks like the tree's trunk is on the ground on the left. It can take 500 years or so for a redwood trunk of this size to decay back into dirt. During that time, it becomes a sort of apartment complex for wild things.

The Back Point Forty hillside, showing Sudden Oak Death and the leaning tree trunks. The pale green leaves are a young Big Leaf Maple. What looks like fog in the background is more dead tanoaks. We could climb the hill to see the ocean, but not get to it. We didn't climb up there for about a decade because of falling trees.

Can you tell which redwood had to be removed?

Here is Donnie, the tree surgeon, at the top of what's left of the tree. He has already removed all the branches, and the top third of the tree. He did an excellent job for us in a dangerous situation.

Donnie is taking another section off the redwood. The house was built too close to the redwoods. Over time, the redwoods are damaged by water running off of the roof.

This picture is taken from the fire road in the Back Point Forty, probably in 2012. I had planted grass. The river is invisible here, behind the row of trees behind the little sun shed on the left.

We called this the guest nest. Brian fixed it up inside with drywall, and it was so cozy, our guests slept forever in there. They had a great view of the river, too, which was behind the building, about 50 feet away. During storms, the water got closer, sometimes only 20 feet away.

The Heart Gardens. Two hearts, side by side, with the path between them. The river is behind the trees, which are behind the sun shed on the left. The driveway is between the gardens and the sun shed.

This photo was taken the second year. This turkey is landing in the spot they all landed, one after another, every morning. Comparing the density of the woods in this photo and the one above of the heart gardens, you can see how Sudden Oak Death changed the character of the property. In the picture above, the turkey would be landing by the points of the heart gardens. Scanned picture.

The original bridge, before any repair work started. I painted it a month before this picture was taken. The wood was so old, the woodgrain had noticeable peaks, with valleys in between that soaked up the paint. Scanned photo.

Here you can see the brick weights hanging on the new wires. The weights are just outside the old bridge because the new bridge is wider. The big wires on a bridge like this are doubled, so if one wire fails, there is still another to depend on. Scanned photo.

The two bridges, old underneath, and new above. We had to climb from one to the other to get across. Scanned photo.

This is the same day as the picture above. The new boards had been painted on all sides before they were put on the bridge. Scanned photo.

Brian is cutting the old bridge wires off the redwood. The tree is no longer constricted. Big sigh of relief from the tree. Scanned photo.

Brian is finally taking down the old tower. Very strong guy! Scanned picture.

The bridge, not quite finished, but straight, flat, and wide, still needs railings.
The dark marks are shadows. Scanned photo.

The bridge support tower on the house side of the bridge. I asked Brian to devise a lattice the plants could grow on, but not interfere with painting the structure itself. I love how it came out. That fern growing everywhere is bracken/jiffy fern. Feels like winter to me but the plants think it's spring, when tea tree and erica bloom in Big Sur, in January and February.

A view downstream. If you think that's a mountain lion stretched out in the water, you'd be thinking just like the deer. It's really a tree stump that hung around, cat-like, for more than a year, and kept the deer away until it washed downstream in a storm. Gardeners, take note.

Five big bucks in the far meadow, unhappy we are watching. This is very soon after the the dead tanoaks were removed.

Our pump set-up. I could fill the water tank, or run any three sprinkler hoses at one time. Each of the hoses was at least 100 feet. The river is pretty high here, and brown. Another foot, and water will be under the pump. Our well tip pipe went from the pump, just to the right of that big red alder, and made it's 90° turn underground further out, nearer to the rushing water.

The alternate version of our water system. Here is our floating bottle at the end of the pipe with the foot valve. Sometimes, the water was so low, we had to scoop out a depression to put the foot valve in to be able to pump at all.

On our way north.

Part 3: Crossing Paths with Wildlife

The Turkeys

I started to feed the birds in the second year of our stay in Big Sur, and there was a new foursome of jakes that liked to chase me back to the house after I spread bird seed around for them. I think maybe the fuchsia-pink bathrobe I wore the first time they saw me upset them, color is so important to turkeys. Jakes are teenage male turkeys, and like all teenagers, they like to test the limits of everything, you know, to see how things work. Jakes, like adult tom turkeys, are about two feet tall, with a very powerful jaw and beak, and incredibly powerful wings and legs.

An adult turkey can jump off the ground with those powerful legs and start flying from that one jump, even though they weigh 18 to 30 pounds. That's really strong. No other bird is that big and even other birds near that size have to get a running start to fly. And a turkey can fly fast, up to 55 miles per hour in a matter of seconds, like a car. They don't fly far at that speed, but they can fly away quickly to escape danger. They are so very smart about body language, they are one of the hardest animals to hunt. Calling these guys birds seems almost insulting, they are so powerful. But these particular jakes weren't our first experience with wild turkeys.

Turns out our first experience was not totally wild. The first turkey we saw was a hen with a baby. The baby was about a third as tall as the hen, but honestly, we had to get the bird book and look it up to know they were turkeys; we had never seen wild turkeys before. Hens are very drab and don't look anything at all like Thanksgiving decorations. I thought they might be bitterns.

I had made the decision not to feed birds there for the first year, even though I was an avid bird feeder. I wanted to know what was going on there naturally before I made any decisions about feeding. So I had no bird food when we first saw the birds we soon called Honey and Baby. We watched and heard them wander around the driveway, and they disappeared. I was enchanted and I thought I would put some bread crumbs out so they could find it next time they came by.

But as I was standing by the driveway, breaking up the bread and dropping it on the ground, the birds reappeared a ways down the driveway, ran straight to me and the hen grabbed the bread right out of my hand. The baby wouldn't do that, so I dropped some more on the ground, but the hen was very friendly and really wanted that bread. It was an instant relationship, she knew immediately we would protect her and her baby, and they hung around for most of the day. And they were there in the morning, too. They were not afraid of our dog Buddy, who was smart enough to understand we were friends with these turkeys because he saw me feeding them.

Let me just say though, if you're not afraid of turkeys, you should be. They can hurt you if they want to. Within their turkey society, life is harsh, with a leader who can not be challenged, but must be challenged, because that's the way they do it, to remain as healthy and tough a group as they can be.

That first year, we only knew Honey and Baby. They came every day, multiple times to our door, like guests coming to visit. We would hear the baby's soft peeping, the constant calling to it's mother, so they could stay together, and then soon they were standing at the door, waiting for us to open it. Honey always took bread from our hands, but Baby never would. It was a funny relationship they had, where the baby seemed smarter than it's mother because it wouldn't take food from our hands.

And it seemed that Honey would have stayed at our front door all day, but Baby wanted to explore, so Honey followed Baby around, even though a more normal situation would have the mother showing the baby around. We saw lots of the normal behavior later, with other birds, so then we were able to see the difference. Honey and Baby became very important to us. They hung around our house a lot, and we thought they felt safe there.

They found a spot that was perfect for dust bathing, and would come there almost every day when the sun was shining on that spot. They would scratch a dip in the sandy dirt, settle down in it and start fluffing their wings to kick up dust. They would use their wings to scoop the dirt up over their backs and then shake their whole bodies, like dogs shaking off water, but they were shaking the dirt down to their skin. They would get all dirty and sometimes would sleep there in the dirt for a while. Then they would get up, stretch, shake all the dirt off, check each other over for bugs, and then slowly head down to the river for a drink.

I have seen small sparrows taking dust baths, and that is the cutest thing to watch. Just darling to see a tiny bird cover itself with dusty dirt. But seeing a giant bird do the same thing imparts a healthy respect for nature. Watching them perform this act really brings the dinosaur thing to mind.

Sometimes we saw them fly across the river to the property there. They'd be gone for an hour or two, then come back and call at the door again. Every time they came, we split two pieces of bread up to feed them, and they came three or four times a day. They were so polite, and it was so fun to hear Baby calling us at the door. This went on for about six weeks.

Invader

Then one Saturday morning, I saw a Yellow Lab running in the river, a dog I had never seen before. Most people in Big Sur don't let their dogs run loose, to keep them from being eaten by mountain lions or run over by cars. And most dogs are employed, protecting their own property, not running around somebody else's place, acting crazy. Protecting home is a hard job, and dogs are truly valued in Big Sur. It's hard to live in the woods without a dog to keep you informed of intruders.

We thought right away that this dog was suburban by the way it was acting. It was going every which way, and having a blast chasing everything that moved, like it had never been off-leash before. We had already started to look for it's owners when we saw the dog run by again with Baby, legs all askew, in it's mouth. I am still so mad about this, I am fighting back tears as I type. We were heartbroken and livid. That was OUR baby. We started searching all around our property, and then the neighboring places for the dog's owner, and we finally found three women, sunbathing topless nearby on private property, with their camp all set up around them. As we got near, that dog came by, without Baby. It was clearly their dog.

We were so mad, their breasts were the last things on our minds, but they were more concerned that we not see those breasts than anything else. We were yelling at them to put their dog on a leash and keep it tied up. They were so worried about their breasts, they couldn't hear what we were saying. Finally, they managed to cover themselves enough to speak, and said they would tie their dog up after we left. We said no, we would stay right there until their dog was tied. We asked what they were doing there and they said they had the property owner's permission to camp, but we knew that was impossible; they were lying. We didn't say anything about that to them, but we told them that their dog had killed a wild turkey for nothing, that their dog was not hungry and had just done that for fun.

We told them it was hard enough for wild animals to survive without being killed by domestic, well fed animals that don't even need to eat them. We told them it was illegal for them to let their dog run loose, even out here in the woods, which is totally true. But they balked at that. We told them if we saw their dog loose on our property again, we would shoot it, which is not true at all. We would never shoot a dog, but it had the desired effect. We went by there again about an hour later, and they had packed up and gone. We never saw them again and our neighbors told us they had not given them permission to be there.

Firebugs

Needless to say, our first couple of experiences with tourists were surprisingly negative. A neighbor soon called us to help him evict some campers who were building a fire in the middle of a small redwood ring of old growth trees. He had a rifle and we showed up with shovels. These kids didn't even have a ring of rocks around their fire, or any campfire tools at all. They built their fire on *top* of the dry redwood duff, which was covering everything, including what they were sitting on. We may be idiots ourselves, but we knew fire safety. We thought everybody knew to be safe with fire, but I guess not everyone was brought up with Smokey the Bear.

Everything around them was dry and ready to burst into flames, and they didn't have a clue about the danger they were in, or how they were endangering others. They had no way to put the fire out. We were surprised our neighbor brought a rifle, but we were glad he did when they declined to put out the fire and go away. He pointed the gun at them, and kept it on them. The three of us watched as the kids put the fire out with one of our shovels and gathered their things, while we explained fire safety. The way they were not tending the fire, the low moisture content of the immense amount of duff kindling everywhere, their fire was ready to spread and could have taken much of the valley with it. This kind of thing is happening more and more, as locals have to defend the forest from an overwhelming number of tourists who feel entitled to leave a mess, and who do not know fire safety, or common courtesy. Big Sur is a dangerous place. If you come to visit Big Sur, please be careful. Educate yourself about safe campfires, and teach your friends, too. Thanks.

Honey's Heart

We were heartbroken about losing Baby, she was the sweetest bird. She *knew* us. but Honey was absolutely devastated. She searched tirelessly for three days, making the most pitiful cry, over and over, and looking everywhere, calling, not eating, rushing from place to place. After that, she stopped coming to our house, and spent her time somewhere up on the ridge top in a gated community where she, herself, had been born. We heard through the grapevine that a guy up there kept birds (chickens, ducks, geese, turkeys) both in and outside aviaries, and Honey was happy up there. Sometimes she would choose to sleep in an aviary and other times she would sleep in the trees above the cages. About a year later we got a chance to go by there to see her and she recognized us and came right up to say hello and take some bread. She was so sweet.

This man is one of the most beloved residents of Big Sur, and has a history of helping the community neighbors and their animals, for planting trees, and liking his privacy. One of his occasional activities was hatching wild turkey eggs, raising them and releasing them to the wild to procreate on their own. Forty or fifty years ago, there were hardly any wild turkeys around the area. Hunters have been doing this across the country to increase the number of turkeys available to hunt, and the program has been a success. He started to put food out for the wild birds, too, and some years later, Honey was born from those birds who came to get food and the ones he raised and released. And she stuck around more than the others.

Company Coming

One evening we were working upstairs when we heard someone knocking on our back sliding glass door, which never happened before. We went down to find a tall, fat, dark, very shiny turkey with a red head, pecking at our glass door. The sun was coming down from the west, and the light was reflecting on the glass door so the turkey saw himself and the trees and the other side of the river, in the door, just like it was a mirror. He was fighting with his reflection, trying to peck it's face. He didn't even notice us behind the glass until we turned a light on. He jumped backwards off the deck and ran straight up the hill. We were pretty shocked by the whole thing.

We didn't really know about the trouble reflections off windows cause birds. We learned a lot living with so many windows (32) and so many trees. We found when the sun shines on a window it reflects whats opposite - other buildings, trees, the sky. When it looks like trees and sky, the birds think they've found a tunnel through the building to fly through, and hit the window so hard, they often die. We found turning our lights on inside helped in the morning and evening, but it didn't stop it from happening during the day. When you do as much as I do to create a haven for birds, knowing your own house is part of their problem is frustrating.

The Northern Pygmy Owl

One time a northern pygmy owl took up residence in our neighborhood, and it was hunting the flock of dark-eyed juncos that were wintering with us that year. According to many bird books, these owls eat rodents, but the juncos can look like rodents, and predators are often opportunists anyway. So for about a month we were witness to an owl stalking the juncos (little brown and black sparrows) as they fed on redwood seeds. Juncos do a little forward and back shuffle on the ground to uncover the seeds, and in the heavy rain years, when there's a large flock, it can look like the ground itself is twitching and wiggling as far as the eye can see. A flock that big is a sight to behold.

The Owl would hunt from branches that were safely hidden in the background shadows of the Redwoods, about 8 - 10 feet above the ground the juncos were wiggling around on. These owls hide so well, I was surprised when I realized what I was seeing. The northern pygmy owl is very small for an Owl, not all that much bigger than a robin, and reddish brown, so it disappears in the red-brown of the redwood forest easily. And this owl had been terrorizing our junco flock, picking off a bird as it took off from the ground to land on a bush branch, you know, to get a better view of the area, to choose another spot with more seeds, or to find their partner.

Juncos are one of my favorite birds, and to see them picked off like that was pretty irritating. I provided birdbaths for them, which they used even though the river was just 35 feet away, so I guess they feel safer at the birdbath. But there was nothing I could do to keep them safe from the owl that had moved in. The owl I encountered was not even intimidated when I was standing 10 feet away and staring straight at it, which was the darnedest thing. Birds don't usually like to be looked at. It makes them nervous, it's something only predators do to them.

But this owl was willing to have a staring contest with me. I'd read that you should never give owls the chance to scratch you, because they are so good at it, so I was nervous about standing so close and staring, but this behavior seemed unreal. Until I looked it up in my Golden Field Identification Guide and saw the owl has coloring that makes it look like it has eyes on the back of it's head, so it hadn't been staring at me at all. How embarrassing, tricked by an owl. Yes, it was just getting dark out and it was in the shadows. Still...I was tricked by an owl.

Who Sleeps Where

A few nights later I was watching a small group of juncos hanging out back on a small redwood that gave them a good view down to the river and up the hillside, where they were roosting (sleeping) in cavities under tree roots. The little birds like to gather together before bed for a chat session, something the Steller's jays and acorn woodpeckers do as well, but the jays and woodpeckers seemed to always be having a vigorous argument instead of the delightful chats the juncos had. We came to think the jays and woodpeckers were arguing about which apartment they would each sleep in that night, but it was just a guess.

From what I can tell, the woodpeckers dig the many nest holes in the trees that are needed for their family's apartments, then the Steller's jays take control of some of them for their own families, forcing the woodpeckers to dig out more nests. But every night, it seemed the woodpeckers were arguing with other woodpeckers and the jays with other jays. They had their knock-down-drag-out fights between species during the day.

Steller's Jays and the Acorn Woodpeckers have similar problems that force them to live in family groups; the teenagers stick around to help with the next generation or two of babies their parents have, because there aren't enough females for the young males to mate with. The "arguments" these birds have every evening are loud, and seem serious. They're often screaming and then there's a slow settling down to quiet. We never saw any actual nighttime fights.

Arguing with Themselves

But often in the afternoon we would see a Steller's Jay alone on a branch, always within an inch of the trunk of a redwood, chattering away, ever so intently, yet quietly, to itself. The birds were so animated during these sessions, we couldn't help wondering if they were practicing what they were going to say that night in the group argument. We were surprised by how often we saw and heard this from our windows. If they became aware of another Jay nearby, they would smooth out their feathers and fly to them, and not let any other bird know what they were doing.

Owl Dust

One night I thought the juncos might be having one of those family conversations about where to sleep, because the hillside is filled with little caves under tree roots, choice places for a group of little birds to sleep. I've seen them feeding their babies in, and flying to and from these cavities. But they weren't doing any of those things that evening, they were acting kind of jittery and nervous.

One of the juncos took a sudden flight past our back sliding doors, and an owl came from out of nowhere to catch that bird. It all happened so fast, but the junco narrowly escaped and the owl hit the glass hard, really hard. It bounced off the glass so hard it left its impression in dust on the glass. It landed about four feet away and landed, miraculously, standing upright on its feet on the deck. It never moved again.

Once I saw the owl, I understood why the juncos had been acting nervous. But the owl seemed alive to me, I mean, I don't know of any animal that dies and remains standing, so I wondered about what to do for the owl. It was getting dark and would be cold that night, like every night in Big Sur, but I was too inexperienced to know what I should have done.

What I did was cover the owl with a fiber pot; it's for plants and it's made of recycled paper that is meant to be buried with the plant's root ball still inside it. It decomposes under ground after it's planted. I had one that would fit perfectly over the bird and because it wasn't really big, would keep the bird warm enough till it recovered. And I thought it would be light-weight enough to knock off itself. I hoped.

While I contemplated what to do, I could see the juncos still fluttering and chattering around the tree they had been on, when a large junco male took a little fly-by of the owl to check things out. The juncos went still and silent as he left the branch, and as he returned to the branch, they burst into happy chatter and fluttering around.

When I stepped outside with the fiber pot, the juncos again went silent, and they watched me cover the owl. The instant the owl was covered, the juncos broke out in a loud, cheerful chatter and song that could only be compared to "Ding Dong, the witch is dead." It was so clear that they were happy about this turn of events. We've seen a lot of bird behavior over the years, and to be able to see such joy so clearly, felt like we were sharing a little secret with Mother Nature.

A few minutes later, the big, brave male junco took another reconnaissance flight over the deck to check things out, and again the juncos were silent while he made the flight, and then welcomed him back like a hero.

Unfortunately, the owl did not survive the night, and I learned from the Big Sur ornithologists who run the Condor program, that the owl most likely died from hypothermia, and that I should have:

1- prepared a cardboard box big enough for the bird to stand in and stretch it's wings fully when it woke, placed a soft towel "bed" inside, and put some small breathing holes in the sides of the box.

2- gently laid a clean hand towel over the unconscious bird and gently picked it up with the towel, and gently put the bird on the soft bed of towel in the box, but do not leave the bird covered with a towel.

3- The box should have been closed and put inside the house, so the bird could warm up, and when I heard it moving around after it woke, I should have waited about 15 minutes, then taken the box outside and opened the top so the bird could escape. *So I Did Everything Wrong.*

I was up very early the next morning to check on the owl, and when I saw it hadn't made it, I put the dead bird on the ground under the tree the juncos had been on, because it's a path foxes use, and I thought they would take and eat the bird. What surprised me though, was seeing another small owl flying franticly around, obviously searching for something. Birds are rarely frantic; it stands out. It was another Northern Pygmy owl, and it searched all along the river banks and around the front of the house, and through the woods.

I saw it searching for hours, and finally it found it's mate on the ground as it flew by our deck. I learned that northern pygmy owls form monogamous pairs to raise their young. The female sits on the eggs in a tree cavity while the male brings her food until the eggs hatch. Then both mother and father care for their hatch-lings, taking turns sitting on the nest to keep the babies warm while the other parent looks for food. Since both males and females look alike, I don't know which of the pair was doing the searching that morning. But it seemed clear to me that this was an emotional event, finding this mate passed away.

This bird made three passes flying over the dead bird, then flew to the branch directly above the dead bird, and sat there staring for a long while. It then flew to the ground and stood so close they were touching, and checked it over very slowly, looked directly into it's face repeatedly, picked at it's chest feathers and then pressed it's body and face against the dead bird for a long while. The bird finally stepped back, took a long last look, and flew away. We never saw another northern pygmy owl there again. And much as this whole series of events breaks my heart, I try to remember, the juncos had lost many members of their family to the owls, and they were thrilled.

Body Language of Turkeys

We got more involved with turkeys because they kept coming to the back door and knocking, or pecking on the glass. The first time, it was just one turkey, but every time they came by, there was another, until there were four giant dinosaurs standing side by side on our back deck, pecking at their own reflections on our sliding glass door. The glass doors were nine feet wide, and the turkeys spaced themselves pretty evenly.

Up until the time Honey came charging at me, and pretty much stole the bread from my fingers, I had what might be called an incredibly healthy respect for large birds. Or you could just call it fear. Honey never acted threatening to me, just hungry, so that helped. But these big guys clearly had violence on their minds. Their bald faces and heads were all red and purple as they pecked at their reflections. Two of them had a strange, noodle looking string of skin that hung down from a center point just under their eyes and above their beak, and they would shake themselves and it would flip, and hang down the other side of their beak.

This red and purple coloring is something that changes with their mood. The more upset they became with their reflections, the redder their heads were, and the longer that noodle thing got. We could see as they arrived at the deck that their heads were pale white and the noodle thing was just a small cone of flesh sticking up, about an inch tall, and as they got involved in attacking their reflection, and got more and more upset, that thing got longer and longer and redder, just like the skin on their heads.

These guys were taller than Honey, and as they faced their reflections, they stood even taller. Unlike Honey and Baby, they were dark, sleek and very shiny, and they had a tuft of what looked like hair, about an inch and a half long, sticking straight out of the center of their chest. It looked like an unfinished body part, or a genetic mistake. But it turns out it's one of the most important signals the birds have; it shows the other birds how old they are. No self-respecting female turkey will mate with a young turkey; males and females mate only when they are both at least two years old, when the males are called Tom and females called Hen. The older a male turkey is, the more knowledgeable he is about mating and leading a group, and I guess that's important or there wouldn't be a tuft of hair advertising it. But they only live about 6 years, and not all males get to mate during their lives.

The Importance of Tuft

This little tuft of hair in their chest is a single feather that never falls out, and it continues to grow longer and thicker throughout the turkey's life, more like hair than like a feather. By the time they are two year old toms, the tuft doesn't stick straight out any more, it now points to the ground, but it's still quite noticeable. It continues to grow, and once it starts dragging on the ground, the ends get broken off, so it never appears longer than that. From a distance, though, you can easily see how old a turkey is by how long and thick that feather is.

These jakes on our deck would occasionally bang their chests against the glass, and we worried they would break the glass. It seemed just as they were getting violent enough to cause a break, they would transfer their anger at their reflections to each other, and go off on a vicious chase through the woods, with a possible attempted attack on each other. I say attempted because, even though they had to determine as a group which one was the biggest and strongest, they still wanted to be all together to show off to the females as a group of four. So they would go off to run circles around a tree, chasing each other round and round, until they ran out of energy and left the circle, one by one, leaving the winner standing. We almost always saw the same guy win, the guy we called Big Daryl.

Between Four Turkeys

We saw them get really vicious, then they would try to jump up so they could land on each other, so to stab with the sharp claw on the back of their legs. Sometimes these fights were between just two, and sometimes all four. These are seriously scary events when you care about the individual birds. Once I tried to stop them from fighting by offering food. I would say they completely ignored me, but it was more like they looked through me; I was insignificant, and it was clear they would run me over if I didn't get out of their way. These are such powerful birds, I wouldn't want to get into a fight with one. They'll strike you with the leading edge of their wings and peck you repeatedly, oh so quickly. Their necks are really strong and their legs and claws are powerful and sharp. They can kill each other with a kick to the head. I don't think other birds can do that.

Teenage female turkeys are called "jennies." Turkeys live in a society where only the largest, strongest, most aggressive male gets to mate. Yes, only one of those big males gets to mate with all the females in the group that year. No wonder they fight. Determining who is the biggest, baddest turkey around is the most important issue of their lives. They work on this every day. It seems every decision they make is based on where they sit in the hierarchy, and what they think their chances of moving up are. The females feign boredom with the antics, but they are watching very, very closely, because it's just as important to them. But it seemed to me that this group had already worked out who would be king before we met them.

Hatched on the Ridge

They came by so often, we had named one of them Danny, so we could sing,"Oh, Danny Boy" to him; he had the darkest feathers. I thought he was the most attractive bird of the four, and he had a "snood," that noodle like thing that hangs down from just above their beak. I mention this because two of the turkeys didn't have a snood, so we wondered if it was a different kind of turkey. I called our local expert up on the ridge and he told me he had hatched and pen-raised these four guys and released them just weeks before we first saw them. He said those two had worn their snoods off by rubbing them on the cage while they were chasing each other around. As I write that, I realize that pretty much pegs them as being the more aggressive of the four. You have to be pretty aggressive to harm yourself in the course of doing your thing. I know, because I'm a gardener.

So we named the two without the snoods Daryl and Daryl, as they seemed exactly alike and we thought we'd never be able to tell them apart anyway. And the lighter colored turkey with the snood was named Henry, so we could say, "Oh, Henry!" We didn't tell them their names or call them by name, we weren't trying to tame them. We only used these names so we knew who we were talking about when we had separate experiences with them.

Big Daryl

It didn't take too long before we could tell the two Daryls apart by behavior, because one of them was clearly top turkey, and he allowed no disrespect from the other guys. He had to be fed first when we held bread out for them, and he felt entitled to take anything from the other jakes in the group, including our attention.

These big "boys" started to come to our house every day and we thought we had a pretty special relationship with them. They had total respect for our house, and never tried to come in the door, even when we opened the door wide. Rather, they would try to charm us into giving them food. They had sort of imprinted on the man on the ridge, so they had experience with humans, but were still wary. They ran away from the back deck often if we accidentally raised our hands or moved our arms too quickly.

It was really special when our human friends came to visit and the "Boys" came by to say hello, and we could show our friends the kind of real live birds we've all been eating for Thanksgiving every year, but had never really seen up close. And I think the turkeys felt the same way about us. They thought we were their special friends, too, and they came to visit often.

The four boys were so young when we first met them, they were inexperienced gobblers, and they didn't even try to gobble until they were in their second year. As they grew, they got more interested in gobbling, and they practiced and got better at it. When one Turkey gobbles, the others are supposed to join in instantly, as if they are one voice. That's the value of having four males in the group, they make a big sound and can be heard from a long distance away, to call the females. And these guys practiced a lot.

They communicate with body language. When the leader wants to leave the area, he stands up and stretches his legs and flaps his wings a few times. Then the others all do the same and follow him where ever he goes. So they must have a leader.

My Favorite Memory

One day the Turkeys were hanging out on the hillside while we were doing some major cleaning projects inside the house. We had the sliding door open, with the screen door closed, and I put on a J. Giels Band CD to get us moving, and we prepared to get to work.

Except we got to laughing so hard, we couldn't get anything done. Every time the J. Giels Band hit a crescendo, the turkeys joined in with gobbles at the perfect moment, like experienced musicians. They happily joined in every song on the album - every chorus, every verse, and didn't miss a beat. We were weak with laughter, and except for getting a VHS camera on them, we didn't get much done that day.

The next weekend, our dearest friends came to visit and we played the tape for them. The turkeys were again hanging out on the hillside above our house, but we didn't have the doors open this time. The tape wasn't that loud, but as we watched it and laughed together, the turkeys heard our laughter and their own gobbles, and gobbled with us. We heard them gobble and laughed again, and they gobbled again, and we laughed again. The longer it went on, the funnier it got and the more they gobbled. We exhausted ourselves laughing, and they got tired gobbling, but the boys stayed there for hours after we all calmed down and they continued to gobble with us every time we laughed. This is my favorite memory of our time in Big Sur, on so many levels.

The Girls Arrive

All of their gobbling was effective, and soon hens started to show up to check things out. There were a lot of hens, too, and when they were all together, the flock was about 25 birds. That's when I started to put seed out for them every day. We couldn't keep feeding them bread. And once the hens showed up, we became insignificant. They stopped coming to our back deck. The boys had so much to learn, and we couldn't help them with any of it.

They all started to roost overnight in the trees up on the hill above our house. First thing in the morning, they would fly over our house to land on our path, which went by a clearing where they liked to gather. I know that doesn't sound like a big deal, but it was a spectacular sight that felt like a big event every time we saw it.

First one to fly down would always be the leader, now called Big Daryl, followed seconds apart by the other Daryl, then Henry, then Danny, and they would all strut and gobble for the hens, but the males were still so young that they didn't yet know how to puff themselves into the full "Thanksgiving position." So they just did their standard strutting around and acting tough thing.

Then the hens would fly over the house and down to the path to join the boys and form a large group in a ritual that reminded us of 1950's WWII fighter pilot movie scenes. The girls were taking off from different perches across a large area high up the hill, flying over our house and converging on a small path. To us it looked like the whole sky was filled with these giant birds, who would then land one after another on the same spot on the path like it was a runway, just seconds apart, like they had been cleared for landing.

They must have been timing themselves, watching just when to take off and land to pull off this accident-free, synchronized performance every morning. And after pulling off a fabulous performance like that, the birds spent some time acknowledging it and congratulating each other; they were proud of themselves and they enjoyed strutting their stuff, saying good morning, checking each other out, looking for bugs and walking to the river for a drink and a stretch of the legs. While they were at the river, I would go outside and start spreading seed around.

The Top Hen

A few hens would stay with me, waiting for food, and one of them got to know me pretty well. If I slept through the morning performance, she would hang out exactly where I would be looking every morning when I first sat on the john and opened the window shade to look out at the river. There she'd be, looking me right in the eye, asking with her expression if I planned to put food out today. I loved that bird. She got to know me better than some of my family. She was the leader of the hens, she seemed to guide the other birds out of harms way; she was aware of the whereabouts of the whole flock, where as the other birds were only aware of themselves and their problems. She was altruistic, and always said thank you.

Animals Say Thank You

Some animals do say thank you for the food you give them. We had a chihuahua mix once who always said thank you. He would find me after he ate, climb up to my chest to look me in the eye and give me his big smile with all his crooked teeth (cutest dog smile, ever), and then be adorably affectionate, pressing his head under my chin and making an affectionate little sound we called "leaking." He was the sweetest little guy. And Top Hen always said thank you, too, always walked by closely, slowly, catching my eye, giving me a little head bow.

Understanding Reflections

The boys had been saying thank you to us for the bread we gave them by hand, by looking us in the eye and nodding their heads at us, but after the hens showed up, they were just too busy to pay us much attention. And by then they had learned that those reflections were themselves, not some other group trying to beat them up. I was watching as Henry came to understand about reflections. The Daryl next to him was attacking his own reflection, and Henry was watching him do that, instead of attacking his own reflection as he usually did, so I could see the light bulb go on for him. Then he looked at his own reflection and turned to see what Daryl was doing again, and as he did that, he caught his own motion in the reflection, and saw himself look at Daryl, and the light bulb got brighter.

After that, Henry stopped attacking his reflection, he just hung around on the deck waiting for bread, and the other boys were able to see that his reflection was waiting around, too, it was not attacking him when it had the chance, and as time went on, they all understood.

The whole flock of turkeys started to spend their afternoons roosting on the hillside in a Big Leaf Maple. These are giant forest trees that aren't often seen in yards in the suburbs. They get to be 80 feet tall and 60 feet wide and the whole thing is giant - giant trunks, branches and giant leaves. Perfect for these giant birds.

If There's a Routine

So the turkeys were in the habit of sleeping at night in the trees on the hillside and waking up to fly to the clearing for their morning greetings. Then getting a morning drink at the river, coming back to the clearing to eat the seed I put out. Then a dust bath and nap on the ground. Then they were off for their walk-about around the neighborhood, then roosting in the late afternoon on the maple again, where they waited for the local guy up on the ridge to come home. He always had some special green foods up there. After dinner they would meet at the big maple for their overnight roost, and awake the next day to start their performance once again.

Turkeys don't see well at night, and they didn't argue about sleeping arrangements that we were aware of. Not seeing well at night is a danger, if they are knocked out of their tree, they are "sitting ducks" for predators. They can't fly back up except on rare occasions of bright moons that break through the forest canopy to light their way.

Transformation on the Hill

One day that giant maple tree came crashing down. The tree was so large that it's branches were intertwined with many other trees. Those branches were breaking as it fell, and the noise was overwhelming, causing a physical discomfort. We had been living there for three years and this was the first big tree we heard fall. The experience was infinitely more frustrating than it would have been just two weeks earlier, before we put shades up on our new double pane windows.

We just couldn't see outside to know which tree was falling, or which way to run for cover. It seems like I ran around the house trying to decide what to do, but I think I was really standing still, trying to decide what to do, trying to hear what to do, trying to hear if the tree was falling towards us when Rick finally made it out the back door, just as the noise pretty much stopped. Rick looked up to see the tips of a smallish branch hit one of the upstairs windows and slide down the pane of glass about a foot, but the glass didn't break.

So, no physical damage to us, just the intense heart racing and facing of death to recover from. Nothing to it, right? I shook for an hour. But the turkeys were not bothered by their sleeping tree changing it's position. The tree was now lying upside down on the hillside, with the top branches now blocking our back door, and a lot of extra dirt flying around in the air, enough to make us go back inside.

Once we got back inside and raised the curtains, we could see the turkeys climbing the hill, jumping up on the upside down branches, and settling down as if nothing had changed. Turns out when a big tree falls in dense woods, it leaves a hole in the canopy the sun can finally get through, and it makes a sunny spot at least once a day on the forest floor. This new sunny spot was on the upside down branches of the Big Leaf Maple, making it the perfect, warm place to roost in the afternoons.

I think the turkeys were thrilled by the whole thing. Their view was improved, their warmth was enhanced, their access to us was better because they could now see us inside our house from those perches. Rick removed the smaller branches with a small, imitation chainsaw (we got a real one later that week), and that improved their access, too. They continued to nap there in the afternoons, but began to roost in trees higher on the hill.

Spring Brings Change for the Turkeys

While the turkeys knew instinctively that they had to fight amongst themselves to determine their leader, and they knew instinctively that they should "strut and drum," they didn't know how to do this mating display very well. They had to practice, just like with gobbling. They had to build up the strength required to do it by doing it over and over again.

This mating display looks like the Thanksgiving turkey decorations we all know and love, which is weird because they only do that display in spring and early summer, not in fall when Thanksgiving is celebrated. Male turkeys don't walk around looking like that all the time, just in front of hens, in spring. But they spend so much time in that puffed up display, strutting in a half circle in front of and around any female they see, they just don't have time to eat.

White Meat

That's why we have white meat turkey breast to eat at Thanksgiving dinner. That extra big breast on the Toms provides all the nutrition they need while they display and mate with the Hens. Without that enlarged breast, they would have to stop to eat and some other turkey would have a chance to get in there and get the attention of a female and mate with her. It's a very competitive lifestyle and that big breast is the most "special power" the males have.

During summer, hens without chicks are checking in and out of all the flocks in the area as they size up each situation and check in with their Hen friends. They're looking for the healthiest males with the best territory, and they like to be with their friends.

Our boys had a pretty good set up even if they were inexperienced, because of our feeding and protection, the river so near, and the highs and lows of our terrain, it all gave them options for heating and cooling themselves, as needs be, and eating and drinking. And our nearby neighbor gave them greens every night at diner. The boys had 20 hens following them through the winter and they (and we) all watched as the boys fought each other and learned to do their display. It was quite a show.

Nothing for You, Dear Boy

But it turns out the hens didn't actually mate with our guys that year. As spring came around, the mature hens left to find other, mature, two year old toms to mate with. And our jakes only got to practice in front of the jennies that were still too young themselves to mate. And they needed the practice.

First our boys learned to spread their tail and lift it straight up behind them. They didn't have other males to learn from so it took them a while to work it all out. They watched each other, though, and tried to out-do each other with the fanning of their tails. That fan sends a message about their age as well. When a mature tom turkey fans his tail, all the tail feathers in the fan are the same height, which is easy to see from a distance, but an immature jake's tail is taller in the center, about two inches taller in the four center tail feathers, which is quite obvious when they fan their tail. It's not a graduated difference, but sharp angles. And hens are picky about this age thing, so it matters.

Hens on the Nest

Most of the Hens were gone for a couple months. After mating, they would find a place to lay their eggs far away from their usual stomping grounds and off the beaten path. They are looking for a place where they can sit on the eggs and be invisible. To one side of a fallen log is a pretty good place, they blend in with a fallen tree.

They lay an egg every day until they have 13 in the nest, which is as many as a hen can cover with her body in a nest. After they lay the 13th egg, they begin to sit on the nest nearly full time, until hatching. Some hens make more than 13 eggs and they will lay the extras in a cache that other hens use as well. One time we found a pile of brown eggs in a really odd place, quite obvious in sand along the side of the river. And there were so many eggs, more than two dozen and they were not covered in the least like a normal nest is. In a real nest, every egg that's laid gets covered with fallen leaves by the hen right after she lays it, and there were no leaves at all in this pile.

We were really thrilled when Top Hen came by one day with her brood, 13 teeny-tiny chicks that were so cute, you want to hug them all. But you can't. You can only watch. She brought them right up to our front deck and they were following so closely, peeping their teeny-tiny little peeps, bobbing up and down as they waddled along, keeping eyes on Mom. She settled very slowly down into a resting position in the warm sun and as she did, all the chicks gathered under her and disappeared under her belly feathers, except one, who had trouble getting hidden and ran around her trying to get under.

She had to make a special lifting of the wing to help and that gave me just a peek of the babies trying to stay close and making room for the one left outside, before she finally settled down. This is what it means to take someone under your wing. They are so cute. She stayed there while the sun was on her, and while she was there, I snuck out the back door and put seed out in the usual spot, which she saw me doing. And when I got back inside, she got up and led them to the seed. It was a long, slow walk.

She had to keep her eyes on the distance, not just in front, but behind and all around to keep safe from predators. And the babies were so tiny they really didn't know what to do. I think it was their first walk out of the nest, as they weren't very good at walking. They made odd little leaps and starts and had trouble with the rhythm of walking and keeping an eye on mom, too, but mom kept her eye on all of them while she watched for enemies.

It's a really hard life for these birds, and it was a difficult year for Top Hen in particular, who lost all her babies early on. I think all wild animals big enough to bite them love to eat baby turkey. By the time a baby turkey is big enough to be called a poult, it has lost most of its siblings. Over the years the largest, oldest family we saw was 3 poults reach adulthood.

Important Alliances

Towards the middle of summer, more hens started to bring their babies around to meet the other hens and their babies, and they would form small alliances throughout the summer of three or four hens and their poults. By fall they joined together and formed a large stable winter flock including Our Boys, (who were tired of displaying), and females, with all the poults having attained near full size, but not near full maturity.

That winter, Our Boys taught the new jakes how to fight and be aggressive by fighting and being aggressive. The Boys fought off all the single jakes in the group that was left, and maintained their superiority, except for a group of four jakes that all looked exactly alike and always came together, so I assumed they were brothers. Those jakes kept hanging around making a nuisance of themselves; they wanted to take over the flock. And for some reason, they didn't like me. But by spring, they knew Our Boys were the dominant guys who would get to mate. It wasn't just that Our Boys beat them at being tough, the hens completely ignored the jakes, no matter how well they displayed.

Mating Day is Always February 14

It wasn't until the next spring we got to see our boys mating, and they did it right in front of our house with us watching. I guess if you grow up on a farm you can see things like this on a regular basis, but we were mesmerized by the show. The mating is cued by the hours of daylight, so in Big Sur they always started the process on February 14. The toms were in display All. The. Time. We saw them displaying 150 feet up in the trees, walking back and forth on big redwood branches, showing off for the hens, before they would even sail down to their morning meeting place.

The mating display involves making all their feathers on their body stand upright at a 90 degree angle from their skin as well as spreading their tail, not just spreading it wide, also lifting it upright to make a half-circle, dark backdrop behind them. It's their own personal stage to show off the beautiful colors their face and head turns when they are aroused. They have bald heads so the hens can see the color changes, and see that snood hanging down over their beak. They go from pale white to pale pink, to dark, dark pink, then on to deep purple, and these colors look almost iridescent. When he's purple, he's ready.

Once they get this part of the display down, they start learning the walk that goes along with it, a special crouching walk that makes their wing tips scrape the ground and make an interesting sound. They hum while scraping their wing tips on the ground, and there is a particular extra clicking sound that they make when they end their half circle, puffed up display, which is synchronized with the sound the dragging wing tips make. It's all rather quiet, just for the particular hen he is dancing in front of. While gobbles can be heard far away, they only gobble to call the hens to them. Once they have a hen to show off to, they focus totally on her to give her their full show.

So we had four Toms ready to mate, displaying every waking minute, and about 20 hens looking for mates, all converging at our house for a party, every day. And it seemed to me that Top Hen was involved in it all. She seemed to be organizing these matings, encouraging, herding the hens to form small groups of two or three to watch the boys display. Big Daryl, the winner of the contest for lead turkey, would be the one to make the half circle directly in front of a possibly ready hen, with his boys at his sides displaying as well. This makes the hen feel pretty tended to. The toms keep repeating their dance until she takes a few steps away, looks over her shoulder at Big Daryl, lets him follow her, then lays down and waits for him to make his approach, which he does by slowly walking up first her tail, then her back, sort of massaging her back with his feet as he goes. That leads to a lot of wing fluttering and panting and somehow amongst all the fluttering and walking, their parts meet and do the right thing.

While the real mating is happening, the other boys are flirting with the other hens, getting them ready for their turn. But the other boys think they might have a chance while the top guy is busy. So Top Tom has to be thorough, but quick enough to keep any of the other boys from having enough time to accomplish anything. We got to see all these interactions play out 10 feet from our front door.

Double Dating

A few days into the mating cycle, Big Daryl had been mating with hens 100 feet down the driveway, after which they all headed to our front yard. The boys were still displaying at any moving thing, and Top Hen was with another young hen near the deck. Everyone in the flock knows the rules about who can mate with who but apparently turkeys like to break the rules, too. It was clear that this one hen wanted to mate with Henry, not Big Daryl, because she kept looking at him and walking in front of him and looking over her shoulder to ask him to follow her. But every time she did this, Henry would look at Big Daryl, and not follow. She came up on our deck in exasperation to be with the Top Hen.

Top Hen had seen everything we saw. We saw the two hens looking back and forth between themselves and Big Daryl and Henry, and soon, Top Hen had gone and offered herself to Big Daryl, (who said yes) but she kept looking at the other hen, then looking at Henry. Soon that hen offered herself to Henry again, but he was so astounded by this, he couldn't act. He had no actual experience, after all. He kept looking at Big Daryl, who had no idea what was going on literally right behind his back. Finally Henry started walking on her back and getting it right just when Big Daryl finished with Top Hen.

Poor Henry was just getting into full-on action and understanding, when Big Daryl came to his senses, saw what was happening and ran over to put a stop to it. He grabbed Henry by the snood and dragged him all the way down to the river, with Henry screaming and the other boys following and squawking and making a ruckus the whole way. Any time a male Turkey can join in a ruckus and a possible attack, they're on it. And all the hens followed. They all flew across the river and ran up the path and out of sight. We saw them hours later, and everyone was calm, acting like nothing had happened.

The Interlopers

After Big Daryl mated with all the hens, they all left to make their nests and we were left with our "Big Boys" and their new competitors, that group of four jakes just a year younger than our boys. These guys did not really know me. They didn't know the routine. When

I was outside, they would chase me back into the house, and that is pretty scary. These are big birds, way scarier than those little guys in the movie "The Birds." So I began trying to sneak out of the house when they weren't around to put seed out. I don't know exactly how they knew, but it seemed to me that every time I went to do that, they would find out and suddenly be there to chase me away. Not so bright, chasing away the source of food.

But the whole situation was changing. The flock was even bigger now, about 40 birds. And with competing toms and jakes, they were fighting all the time, and fortunately, they would chase themselves out of my view. These fights are really vicious. We saw many, many fights of a funny nature though, with the boys running in a circle around and around the trunks of big trees, trying to catch each other and inflict pain and damage. They are really serious, but you can't help laughing at a group of 8 red-headed turkeys running around a tree. Just don't interfere. They'd be just as happy to tear you up with those swords they have on the backs of their legs. They have such strong legs, they can jump up high and inflict a lot of damage on the way down. Turkeys legs are so important to them for all their actions, and we could see this clearly when one of our Boys showed up with a bad leg.

Oh Danny Boy

I was surprised to see Danny at our back door without the other boys, but there he was early one morning, before I had a chance to put food out. And it was different to see him actually leaning on the glass. As he saw me, he jumped off the deck and I could see he couldn't use his leg as he tried to flail away. We never got close enough to see exactly what was wrong, and he never got better. But he limped, and sort of dragged his leg; he didn't put full weight on it. For at least two weeks, we didn't see him with the other Boys.

I started to put food and water out back just for him. We saw him with the Boys a few times after that, but he was never the same. This was really hard for me, much as I was willing to help him, get him to a vet to set his broken bone, he just would not let me near him. He was really sensitive about motions we made with our hands and would try to run away if I forgot he was there and started talking with my hands. So when we saw him coming, we would be as still as we could while he was leaning on our glass door, and make our motions slow. That's hard for me to do, I pretty much crash and bash through life. We thought he missed his brothers, and his reflection was the best he could do instead. His reflection never attacked him, but it gave any predator going by the impression there were two turkeys there, not just one to fight. I think Danny was quite clever.

When he was with the Boys, he was at least eight feet behind them, and he did not let them see him limp. If they turned around enough to see him, he would stop moving. One of the reasons Turkeys seem so smart is because they have a 270 degree field of view, which is quite a bit of peripheral vision, almost behind them. So Danny had to keep his eye on them closely so they would not turn around and pick on him. They were not really nice to him. Not that they had ever been nice to each other. They were not.

But they had an "understanding" that as a group they had a better chance of success at everything. Danny was always the low man on the totem pole, the order of which I think was Big Daryl, Henry, Little Daryl and then Danny. But it was a "family" thing - the Boys would pick on Danny themselves, but would fight off any other Turkey that tried to pick on him. They protected him (and me) from the four jakes and I can attest that is damn fine protection. But, like Danny, I was never sure when they might decide to peck at me. What we never figured out was if the boys would fight hard enough amongst themselves to hurt or kill each other. I thought they were more like dogs, and kids, testing strength but not intending to do lasting damage. Or do I have kids and dogs wrong?

A Turkey with a bad leg is in a bad spot. They need those legs to jump off the ground to fly away to safety, or to get to a safe roost. Flying away quickly is their main strategy for how they protect themselves from danger. They also need to spend a lot of time walking around to find food. They fight off rivals with the spurs on the back of their legs. When they use their wings like cudgels to bash their opponent they need two legs for support. And when they jump up to kick a rival turkey in the head to kill it, they need two legs for balance. It's a hard life for Turkeys.

Danny's visits became fewer and more far between, and one day we realized we hadn't seen him in a long while. Life went on. But I still think of him as the sophisticated one. Well dressed and gentlemanly in his darker, shinny "suit." Never started trouble. Always said thank you. Since he was low man, Danny was always the last to leave the deck, and he would always do a little half turn/shuffle and catch my eye, and it felt like he was saying a special goodbye to me. I liked to imagine he was saying, "So long, and thanks for all the fish," but, as I was writing this, I realized he was probably just checking the area behind him for trouble.

Turkeys have a variety of body language cues for each other, and clearly, I don't understand them all. But what I saw was a lot of the same things, day after day. Big Daryl would stand up, stretch, and flap his wings, and within seconds, the other boys were doing it, too. Then they would all march off to their next adventure. Those guys were so very good at imitating him, no matter what he did. Their lives are very synchronized, and the only way I can understand it is thinking about dancing. I can follow my lead partner easily if he leads. And I can lead, too, if I have the opportunity. I don't much, but I think it would be fun, so I pay attention to both requirements.

I don't really want to be the one that always has to lead the dance, though, so I'm willing to let someone who shows he can do it well, do it. So maybe that's sort of what's happening with these guy groups, and girl groups, too. The hens had their own leader, who stopped all fights, and hens fight a lot more than I thought they would. If the Top Hen couldn't stop a fight, Big Daryl would go over and get between the contestants. He is so much bigger than a hen, they followed his suggestions, so to speak. Top Hen would decide who stayed and who didn't stay in the group, and she kicked out interlopers that she didn't want in the group, by chasing them away. Each of the hens have their own personality, some scared and some brave. But they all want to be part of a group.

Scorpions

Within the first month we lived in Big Sur, I was getting a shower at some unnaturally early hour so we could get Rick back to the Bay Area for work for the day. Two days a week I drove while Rick worked in the car, and while he worked in the office, I was getting our supplies at the many wonderful stores in the Bay Area. Monterey County, with less than 500,000 people, is not the shopping mecca the Bay Area is, with their 7.5 million people, so this schedule worked well for us for the first 10 years or so.

Anyway, I was first to step into our brown, sunken bathtub that morning, and when I looked down to the faucet handles I thought I glanced at a scorpion in the tub, about two inches away from my foot. It was nearly invisible on the brown tub, but I froze and very calmly told Rick I thought there was a scorpion in the tub.

Nearly the entire bathroom was dark brown, tub, sinks, counter tops, and redwood walls, all brown. I started wondering, where are the other scorpions, and how many are there? And what is it doing here, anyway? I thought scorpions were desert dwellers, this is the woods. It took a lot of nerve to take my eyes off that one to look around to see if there were others. But I was wide awake now, no need for coffee. Fortunately, I saw no others where I was planning to put my foot. And I got slowly out of the tub.

We decided to kill it with hot water, which was so handy, but realized in the process the guy was stuck in the tub and couldn't get out, just like the other spiders we found there. We found five scorpions in the house that year, and we kept three of them in an small aquarium with dirt and leaf litter in the bottom. I fed them spiders (never a shortage of spiders) that we killed or stunned somehow without smashing, and put in the aquarium. We wanted to know more about scorpions, none of the reference books we had told us enough.

I was able to catch a live spider for the first scorpion and that gave me the chance to watch how the scorpion tricked the spider into getting eaten. I had thought there would be an epic battle between the two, or at least a chase, but no. Once the scorpion saw the spider, it immediately hid, then, out of sight of the spider, buried itself in the inch and a half of leaf litter and sand at the bottom of the aquarium, but it stuck one claw out. The one claw looked and acted like a wounded earwig, flopping about a bit, and soon the spider was checking that "earwig" out. That's when the scorpion popped out and caught the spider with both claws. A scorpion pretending to be a wounded earwig, so even insects are involved in misdirection and misrepresentation of themselves. Deception - it's not just for humans.

We noticed that these three scorpions we collected were fatter than some others we'd seen and we guessed they were pregnant. Unfortunately, we missed the live births, but it was pretty astounding all the same. One day one of the scorpions had a bazillion microscopic, white scorpions on it's back, and a few walking around her, looking for a place to climb on. Within a week the other two scorpions had their babies, too. Really wish I'd gotten to see the births.

But now we had a problem, not just a curiosity. We had intended to watch them for a bit and then release them back into the woods. But we were not comfortable opening the aquarium to put spiders in there with all those babies, and we didn't want to catch as many spiders as they would all need. And we wondered if we would regret releasing them all into our own yard. There were so many.

I thought some natural history museums might be interested, but I could not find a single natural history or school group who wanted them for exhibits. Who'd have thunk it? So we kept them as they were and never opened the aquarium again. I added water through the screen top, and the babies slowly disappeared. We don't know what exactly happened to them, if the adults ate them or they just didn't have enough food to survive themselves, but we found no dead bodies. We finally took the whole thing outside to the Back Point Forty, used a stick to knock the lid off and let the three of them get away. I felt bad about the babies. On the other hand, I'm really, seriously happy none of those babies were born loose in our house. I shiver just thinking about that.

Funnily enough, our friends and family were not as fascinated by the scorpions as we were. We were telling some visiting friends about finding the scorpions when they, looking around worriedly, asked what kind of places they would be likely to find them. I said they liked to hide between layers of material, because I found one between blankets on our bed, but I pointed to a lined curtain as an example. We were all pretty shocked to see a scorpion right there, between the curtain and the lining, just where I had randomly pointed. We were beginning to be afraid they

were going to overrun us. But it was apparently just a one time
population explosion, and most years we just saw one or two in the
house, but I killed at least one every time I was working in the garden for
more than an hour.

Seems they are not the scorpions of our youthful visions, who
grow into giants, and fight and kill humans and pets. The largest one we
saw was only about two inches long. Most of them were afraid of us, and
we found inside the house, we could easily catch them with an old VHS
tape box that had the opening on the short end. Inside the box, they had a
hard time climbing the sides. We just had to keep shaking the box a little
bit to get them to fall back to the bottom while we carried them outside,
and far away from the house to let them go. Or to the sink and the hot
water. Every once in a while, a scorpion would decide to take us on and
fight back, and the fear/excitement that rises from your heart to your
throat during a situation like that is pretty embarrassing. But I got stung
only once in all that time, and Rick never got stung. So it's not much of a
problem. It was less painful than some bee stings I've had, and way less
painful than a medical procedure, or smashing your thumb with a
hammer.

The Deer Bell

We had never lived in a place where we might see deer outside
our window, but there they were, munching on some giant clover,
looking around a bit nervously, but not actually stressed. There was a doe
and two fawns with spots that glowed brightly when the breeze rustled
the trees and a streak of moonlight was able to break through the canopy
to shine light on them. It was so quiet, we could hear them munching. We
had only been in Big Sur a few months, and we were so excited, we
couldn't move or take our eyes off of them, watching as their ears rotated
around so they could hear what was going on behind them. They were
symbols of the love of nature that brought us here. They were so
peaceful and pure. But it was the use of technology that brought about
this particular natural experience.

We had installed some X-10 motion sensors (one of the first
DIY security systems) on the path, thinking we would prevent any future
occurrences of the event that happened a few weeks before, when we

heard some crashing through the bushes-type sounds early on a Sunday morning. We weren't quite awake when Rick jumped out of bed and started to put his jeans on so he could go check it out. I think he had one leg up in the air, half in the pants, when a bright flash went off, clearly from a camera.

We lived in dense, dark woods with no one around and no curtains on our windows, and someone had just taken a picture of the house with probably a clear view of Rick putting his pants on. Put another way, an intruder had trespassed on our property and taken a picture of my nearly naked husband before 9am on Sunday morning. We couldn't believe it. They probably didn't know he was in the picture, they just took a picture of our pretty house. We still hope they didn't get the picture blown up.

Funny as that was, it was still something we wanted to avoid, tourists wandering around our house, taking pictures. We're privacy nerds. We moved to the woods to be alone. (Yes, I do see the irony of being a privacy nerd and writing about my life.) So we got our X-10 system up and running, and set it to ring a delightful bell when anyone walked toward our house. We had no idea how many deer came through until those bells started ringing.

And it was really fun for a while to be awoken in the dead of night to what we soon called the "Deer Bell." We could tell by the ring which path the deer was on, and we got to see some interesting deer behavior. Just looking out the windows we got to see deer being protective of each other, nuzzling each other, congregating together, checking each other out, being affectionate, things they don't do when they think people are watching. Apparently, we had a deer meet and greet place between the house and the cabin, and sometimes we saw as many as 25 deer at a time in the darkness.

We were surprised to find the deer would run away from our two little 12 lb terrier/chihuahua mix dogs. One time we saw a large group of deer, more than 20, straggling through the far meadow on their way to the river, when our little dogs caught sight of them and took off after them. Most of the deer ran off to the river, but there were two small deer lagging behind the group, half an acre away. Suddenly, a very large buck came back from the direction all the deer had run to, and he stood tall in the meadow and faced the dogs as they ran, barking, to him.

Big Buck Protection

The dogs had been chasing the deer for years, and they'd never had one turn and face them like this before, so this was strange behavior and it made the dogs slow down their advance. We could see the buck kept looking back over his shoulder at the two small deer, but they were afraid to move because of the dogs. Multiple times they looked from the dogs to the buck and back again. Finally the buck's message got through to them; they bolted to the river, and as soon as they passed behind him, the buck took off and followed them to the river.

The dogs stopped in their tracks, they had accomplished their goal. Besides, there was some delightful deer poo treats right there for them, a fabulous reward for chasing the deer and their ticks away from the house. They never really understood why we didn't want them to eat this most special treat, or why we never gave it to them in the house; I think whoever packages this "treat" and gets it on the market will have a big success. And I guess what they say is true - the best defense is a great offense. No other deer ever turned around to chase the dogs. But deer are happy to take on people that piss them off.

I know that because Rick tried to film a young 2-point buck that had been hanging around in front of the cabin. He was quietly following the buck when it stopped and turned around to face Rick, and look him straight in the eye. Rick lowered the camera. They were about 20 feet apart. He looked Rick in the eye and pawed at the ground with his right front paw. Rick froze and the buck took a small step forward and pawed the ground again. He was making a clear threat to Rick, and Rick backed up. To have an animal turn to face you head on will make your heart race. Being able to read body language is a survival skill. Challenging us straight on is something turkeys, skunks, and raccoons will do, though, and we, and our dogs, had experiences with them all.

Over 21 years living there, we had a number of dogs, and Missy was the toughest. One night she asked to go out late at night, as usual before bed, but instead of peeing and coming back inside, she took off toward the river's edge, barking her head off, through some thick spooky space to a place we couldn't see. But we could hear the screaming and it sounded like a group and it sounded like someone was getting killed, and we didn't know who.

The sound of bloodcurdling screams scared me stiff. I mean, I froze, but Rick had the opposite reaction, and he took off, barefoot and naked, tearing through the spooky space in the woods to find her. Before he even got there, it got real quiet and I feared the worst, but he found Missy alone and triumphant on our side of the river and five raccoons staring back at him from the other side. She only weighed 30 lbs. We've heard about groups of raccoons capturing and drowning dogs, so we were pretty impressed. But not nearly as impressed as I was by Rick taking off like that at the sound of those screams. Rick had more wounds from running through blackberry than the dog did. In fact, we didn't find a scratch on her, but I got to examine Rick's body closely, and spend quite a bit of time applying ointment to Rick's scratches, and I didn't mind a bit.

Russells for Rodents

The reason we had the dogs, though, besides loving dogs, was to keep the rodent population down. I'd heard about Jack Russel's hunting abilities so I started researching, and we ended up getting some dogs that had no interest in killing rodents, while others were naturals. But we didn't start out thinking we wanted to kill all the rodents. We didn't think about them at all until they became a problem and we had to think about them.

The first rodent exposure we had was the two little mice we found standing on their hind legs, hugging each other, pressed into the last corner of the shed we were tearing down. That corner was all that was left of the 8 x 16 foot shed, and those mice were frozen in place, shaking like leaves. They wouldn't leave, even though we gave them ample opportunity. We finally shooed them out with a broom, and they disappeared into the duff.

We'd read a guesstimate/study claiming there are about 3000 rodents per acre in the woods, and we had two acres, so, we had a rodent problem. And it was a problem inside our house, too. The foundation was a ring of concrete and the rodents only had to dig a tunnel down about a foot to get under the foundation and be under our house. Apparently, they built some sort of hidden super highway somewhere we couldn't find, and so there were rodents in that house every day we were in it. We could hear them walking around inside the walls.

A new type of trap was just out on the market when we moved in, I think it was called the Mice Cube, a trap that caught the mouse without killing it, so you could release the mouse later, outside. We were into that trap. We found out that mice can swim, and so we took the mouse, still in the trap, to the edge of the river. There, because of the box shape of the trap, I was able to gently launch the mouse to land about halfway across the river, and we'd watch it swim to the other side. We took our dog, Buddy, with us., and we sang "Take me to the river, drop me in the water..." every time we did that. Which seemed like a lot.

We only lost one mouse on the river bank. We watched as the mouse turned around in the water and started swimming straight toward us. We couldn't believe it. The mouse ran up the bank, straight at us, and I was able to use the arch side of my foot to sweep it back into the river. But it came back, I swept it back again, and it came back a third time. But this time, it got smart and headed straight for Buddy, and we never saw it again. Like magic, it disappeared in Buddy's long belly hair and managed to get away. Buddy couldn't find it either.

I've thought about this mouse over the years. For all I know, that mouse could have clung to Buddy's fur long enough to make it back into the house; it was so determined to get back to land, none of the other mice had done anything like that. Could it have had babies in the house?

True Environmentalist?

I had a hard time coming to grips with life and death in the woods. I want to see myself as a kind and caring critical thinker, and a good steward to the land, and not one to fall for ideology. Basically, I didn't want to screw anything up. I had always thought the best thing for me would be to leave this earth without leaving a mark.

I especially didn't want to kill anything in this rare environment, not bugs or plants or birds or animals or rodents. But having that as a goal and actually living up to that goal are two different things. We didn't want to kill rodents, they are so cute, and they are just trying to live their lives, too. So who are we to interfere? But with the mice, I had to become more practical. The mice we forced to swim to the other side of the river paid us back by taking up residence in our cars, eating the emergency food supplies we had in there, building elaborate nests with our tissues, and chewing our wiring. Turns out car wiring repairs are really expensive. And we thought we had been so clever in finding a way to not kill them but remove them from our lives.

But they are so darn cute, it's really hard to want to kill them. When I see the trouble they go to just to survive, I want to help them, not hurt them. These little guys shred redwood bark to make soft bedding, or tear tissues into just the right size strips that can be bunched together and not get flat; hard work for just a few nights of softness. And they think ahead, too. They stash food in multiple places so they have it later.

Mouse Party

I once tried using a mouse trap that claimed to catch multiple mice at once, a metal device that said it could hold eight or more live mice. I had read that they often explore in pairs, and will call in their family when they find a good food source. I thought if I used one of these traps with some good bird seed and peanut butter, I could catch a whole family at once. And I did, I think. Well, all I can really say is I saw a mouse in the trap before I went to bed, and when I got up, there was no mouse, and no food in the trap. Apparently, when a whole mouse family gets together, they can work out an escape plan. I imagine the one guy I saw called in his friends and they had a party in this terrific, rain and predator proof mouse restaurant with it's great menu, and I imagine the guy who came late to the party, after all the food was gone, held the door open for the others to leave and followed everybody else out. So I think it's not really a mouse trap, it's a test to see how stupid you are, and if you fail, like I did, you buy the trap.

It was such an expensive trap, I tried it again, and had the same results again, proving I can be both stupid and crazy. So it was essentially a mouse feeding station that provided a secret lesson on how to shop. Now I try to think of all the ways a product might fail to work before I put my money down.

There is a different, multiple-live-mouse trap that says it "spanks" the mice into the chamber, so that trap sounds like it might be escape proof. At least there is no way for one mouse to hold the door open so another mouse can leave, but the real problem is what to do with a little cage full of mice once you have it. Drown them? How awful. I mean, I've done that, and I'll never do that again. Never ever. A horrendous way to go. There's a lot of "country," or "old time" advice on the Internet about how to trap rodents that involves drowning. I don't do that. That's a trap door to hell.

Over the years we were able to plug up more and more holes under the house, and reduce the number of mice visiting us. But toward the end of our stay, the heater vent in our living room was designated a busy International Rodent Portal/Transfer Station, and rodents seemed to arrive every 20 minutes, often in pairs. Seemed to anyway; really, it was one or two every night for a few nights, until the whole family was caught. Then nothing for months, then cycle again.

I found there are two major brands of snap-trap, and one has a bigger spring than the other, and it makes a difference - I once saw a mouse pull itself out of a snap-trap that had the smaller spring, and limp away, a real mighty mouse. That's heartbreaking and inspiring at the same time, but also, a waste of money for the trap, and pretty cruel to the mouse, too.

And mouse lives are hard enough. When you think about it, just about every other species will eat mice like snacks, which gave me the idea to remove the mouse bodies from the traps for other animals to eat, and boy, did they. I don't know exactly who ate the dead mice I left out at night, probably skunks, raccoons and fox, but one time I removed a mouse from a trap during the day, while a crow was nearby, and it saw me leave the mouse on a log bench, in plain sight. The crow swooped down and took off with the mouse, and came back the same time the next day; I hoped it would. I just happened to have another mouse, and so a relationship developed.

Crows and Local Migrations

There was a family of crows who would come to the river every spring, with their babies, to teach them to bathe in the river and search the river banks for food, but only in the spring. That does coincide with the spring population explosion of mice and voles, though. I don't know why the crows weren't around all year, they are resident, not migrating birds. Maybe they migrate locally up and down, from riverside to ridge top, depending on the weather. Could be they spend their summers in the parking lots, where people leave trash that often has food in it the birds will fight over. The resident deer and Steller's jays migrate locally, spending winters on the ridge tops, in the warm sun, and the summers by the river, in the cool shade. But mice spend most of their lives in a small radius from where they were born, just a 100 square feet or so.

Loud Mouth Mice

One day we could hear a high pitched, repeating noise in the living room that we thought might be some weird phone line buzz, because there was a phone hookup right where we heard the noise. Our house needed a LOT of work, and one of the things it needed was better trim around the floor in the living room. So when we looked closely, we could see a tiny mouse stuck under the edge of the drywall, behind the trim, screaming, and it seemed to be trying to flee in fear, but from what, we couldn't see, we could only hear some scratching behind the mouse. But there was nothing we could do to help, and I didn't really want to know what, exactly, might be chasing it under our floor. We banged around on the floor to try to scare the chaser away, but that didn't help.

The mouse was making such a racket, we decided to leave the house and not listen to a rodent possibly being killed, so we went for a walk. When we got back, it was quiet and the mouse was gone, no bloody mess was found. We were surprised by how loud a mouse could scream, though, and it made clear how a mouse could call family to come when they find a great cache of food. When we researched who might be chasing this mouse, we found that Norway rats would eat a mouse, but the dusky-footed wood rat, native to the area (and who had a nest bed on top of the water heater), only eats plants and shares burrows with other rodents, so that couldn't have been the attacker. But it could have been another mouse, defending it's territory. We never solved that particular mystery, and we never saw a Norway rat there. There are other things it might have been, though I don't want to think about snakes. Not snakes in my house.

We All Want to Survive

There are many studies that show how smart animals and birds are, how they can recognize individual people, even when those people wear costumes, and lots more, which I'm sure you can find with an Internet search, if you care to look. Here's what I believe from my experience living on this planet, observing animal behavior, and keeping pets of all kinds, including bugs, as well as reading about the many animal behavior studies. - All living things must survive, and they know how to do that or are in the process of figuring it out. So if you try to kill a spider, it will run away, and if you corner it and try to smush it, it will crouch down and try to hide to avoid your smush.

A spider has to know when it's being chased, has to be able to pick out actions by individuals meant to cause it harm, and has to know when other's actions do not mean to cause harm. A spider has to know when all other species mean it harm, not just other spiders, but it has to be able to pick out that a bird means to eat it and that some other animals want to eat it and humans want to smush it. But most dogs don't care one way or the other, so it's good for a spider not to waste energy trying to avoid an animal that doesn't mean it harm. Every living thing has to nourish itself in some way, remove waste in some way, find a place to sleep and carry out family functions, and interact with others to do those things.

All species need to know these same things to survive. Emotions come into play because of this need to know what other's intentions are towards us. Emotions are Mother Nature's built in instructions to behavior that guides us to survive, which means reproduction for some, care-taking for others, but also knowledge for getting along with all other individuals any species may encounter. Knowing if another means you harm requires reading body language, and body language is pretty much the same, no matter what species you are. If you know what happy looks like in one species, it's easier to see it in others. The raised head, stiff neck and vibrating tail of a rattlesnake ready to strike is so similar to a dog with stiff neck and legs, with a tail that is wagging so stiffly and with such a small arc that it almost vibrates instead of wagging, yeah, they both mean the same thing -- Back off.

The same way that hearing a rattlesnake's tail rattling causes fear (an emotion) to rise from our hearts to our throats, which causes us to be careful; hearing a baby cry causes us to care (an emotion) about why the baby is crying. Worrying about the baby's care is not just natural, it is the sole reason the baby survives.

The course I took from Cornel Ornithology Lab, on Bird Biology, shows a drawing of dots a parent bird sees in the back of their babies throats when the babies open their beaks so wide to be fed. And it's really the same mechanism at work - the same way we know a red-faced, crying baby is really hungry, the juncos know if their babies are opening their mouths wide enough to see those dots, they must be famished.

When we see human babies red-faced from crying, we feel both sorry for the poor hungry baby, but more important, feel a need to fix this problem of being hungry. That's how emotions and survival are so intertwined, especially so for species that care for their young for a long time. And that's why it can be considered a (mental) illness if you don't understand what these cues to body language mean, or don't make the appropriate cues for others to read.

Belted Kingfisher

Every time we sat by the river's edge to relax, we saw and heard the kingfisher. They certainly live up to their name. They are loud, raucous birds who take no crap from anyone. They are elegantly dressed in gray suits and white shirts, with black and white "trim" on the suits. The male wears a fancy brown belt, hence the name. Both males and females have an expressive double crest. They defend a section of the river year round in Big Sur, and we could see and hear the fights that broke out over their perceived territory. These birds patrol their section of river, looking for interlopers, and food. They are constantly trying to steal food from another's territory, that's why they have to be so vigorous defending their own. And they are always trying to expand their territory.

They are pretty astounding to watch, too. They hover or perch above a still pool on the side of the river they can see into, getting the light just right. They totally focus on that spot, and when a fish passes, they dive straight down at full speed, beak first, catch the fish and turn around under water so fast, they don't smash into the bottom, then fly right back up to their perch. They can do this in surprisingly low water.

Then they have to toss it around and catch it head first to be able to swallow it, because fish won't go down the bird's throat tail-first. They put on quite a show, no matter what they're doing. We saw them cheating, too, flying over land to get to the other side of the bend in the river, and doing it so quietly, too, so unlike kingfishers. I shouldn't call this cheating, it was really a sneak attack on another's territory, coming in from the side, sneaking around the border. And their airspace for this sneak attack was well known, I think, because I often saw kingfishers pass each other in the air over our clearing and both make immediate u-turns back to their own side. And without a sound.

Mergansers and Mating Golden-eyes

Before SOD (Sudden Oak Death) killed off the oak under story, and the forest was still so thick you couldn't see more than 10 feet away, we saw Golden-eye Ducks hanging out on the river behind our house. Our stretch of the river had dense woods on both sides and no business use for a long way up and down stream. It was actually quiet, and because of that, we saw a lot of wildlife in our first years there. These ducks are really beautiful elegant birds. Goldeneyes are sea ducks that also spend their winters along the coast's rivers and they nest in tree cavities, as do the Common Mergansers.

It can be hard to tell these ducks apart because they are so similar in coloring. Both species have green headed males and red-headed females. Both species have gray-bodied females and white and black bodied males. Only the female common merganser has a crest at the back of her head, and only the male Goldeneye has a white spot on it's cheeks. The real trick to telling them apart is the bill. The merganser's bill is long, thin, serrated, and light colored. The goldeneye's bill is short and dark. Although we saw more Mergansers than any other duck while we lived there, we never got to see them mate.

Both these species of ducks had been wintering in our neck of the river. We saw them going up and down stream in mixed groups when the water was high and moving so fast, it was hard for us to tell exactly who they were, they look so similar. I've never been white-water rafting, but they made it look like fun, even though it was clearly dangerous, there was so much tree debris in the water. We still wonder how these diving ducks found food when the water was so brown we couldn't see through it.

As the rains stopped, the water slowed and the level lowered, we could see them gather in smaller groups of just males and just females, and closer to mating time, the Mergansers separated from the Golden-eyes. The courting we saw by both species was charming. A male would pick a female out of the group to follow closely; soon he would convince her to separate from the group and go off with him for a time.

The amount of time seemed variable. We would see them working their way upstream, working hard, looking for food, then floating downstream, very close together, being what I would call affectionate. Maybe this was their way of testing their synchronicity together, the way hawks and ravens fly in tight formation together as a way of courting, and the way people dance.

It seemed to me they did a lot of dating, a lot of checking each other out. By the time the water lowered in the spring and the rocks appeared, the ducks had all made their choices and stayed together as couples, and we mostly saw pairs after that. There were always more females than males, and females without mates would group together after all couples had formed. One year, we got to see the Golden-eyes mate.

Ducks mate like all birds, in that you never get to see parts fitting together, just a lot of wing flapping and one bird on top of the other. But this whole process of courting was so much cuter than the turkeys mating dance. Turkeys seem so lustful compared to these dating ducks. Maybe it's because this couple was all alone, there was no group of ducks watching or waiting for their turn, and they didn't know we were there, either. It was like peeking into their private bedroom. This was sweeter than any other bird mating I've seen. We watched them swimming around in a very slow-moving area, together, his neck often touching hers, doing synchronized moves very close together, then they each went to a rock about 10 feet apart and did some grooming, cleaning and fluffing their feathers.

He finished first and swam up to face her, looked into her eyes, and gave a happy little wiggle/giggle with his body. He swam to her tail and charmingly plucked at it once while she looked over her shoulder at him. He swam up her other side to look her in the eye and giggled again. He circled and plucked her tail and charmingly looked her in the eye three times, and each time she look back approvingly. The last time he swam back there, he hopped on her back and the magic happened. Then he swam back to his rock to rest and she stayed on her rock and they groomed themselves a bit. After a couple of minutes he swam back to her and they swam off together.

I don't know how long this whole event took. It seems we were motionless for a very long time, but being motionless can make time stand still, so there is no way of knowing. We didn't see them again that year or any other. We don't know if they did that multiple times, or if that one time was enough. We didn't see any babies. And even though we never saw the Merganser's mate, we did see baby Mergansers, usually one brood a year, sometimes two or three families at once.

Baby ducks are like baby turkeys, both tasty eating for other animals and birds. We saw the Merganser's hatched eight to thirteen ducklings every time, but three was the largest number of baby ducks to reach adulthood we ever saw, and usually it was one or two. I recently read that their reproduction numbers are down, and what we saw over the years lines up with that.

Watching baby Mergansers is so much fun. They are so tiny and fluffy, so spotted, so cute, and so hungry. We didn't get to see how the babies get from the nest to the water, but once they are all assembled, they climb on her back and she swims off. She has a lot to teach them.

I saw a young family at what seems to have been very soon after they got in the water for the first time, and pretty early in the morning, too. I was at the river's edge to make sure the water pipe intake was under water. Just as I was about to come out of the brush and step in the water, I saw a female Merganser in the deeper water upstream, and she had so many babies on her back, I couldn't count them all. The babies were the tiniest I'd seen, and I'd never seen babies on a duck's back before. Scorpions, yes, but not ducks.

She swam to the deepest part of that section and dove underwater, and the babies began swimming frantically in circles, looking at the water, seeming very upset and making baby bird frantic sounding peeps. And then she came up on the other side of the deep water and the babies swam quickly to her, and got on her back with great relief. When they were all calmed down, she swam back to the deep water and submerged again, and she repeated the whole process 3 times before I had to get back inside the house.

We spent the next week looking every chance we got for the baby ducks to see their progress. It seemed to me they were diving underwater themselves later that day. They were still spotted as they grew and followed their mother up and down stream all summer. Every sighting was fun.

The adult Mergansers swim purposely upstream, diving and eating small fish, bug life, frogs and salamanders as they go. Then they rest while they float downstream. When they get to their favorite turning point, they turn around and swim upstream, eating again as they go. But the babies don't just swim with purpose, like the adults, they are flying underwater as fast as they can, in a competition with their siblings for nutrition because they are growing so fast and are so, so hungry. They can't wait to be adults.

I don't know exactly how the babies can swim so fast, but they speed through the water from side to side while their mother is taking her time. You can see from the intent in their speed and direction that they are chasing food underwater, changing direction on a dime. They are everywhere at once. All summer. It seemed any time we were outside more than a half an hour, we had the pleasure of watching the babies competition for food.

We don't know if the Mergansers had a certain section of the river they defended, the way Kingfishers do, or if they just let their appetite decide for them. But we saw them a lot. As fall came, the babies were adult size and coloring, and as far as I could tell, they all looked the same, like females. They started to form large groups with other females and their young, and by late fall the males and females have turned into their breeding colors and we could tell the difference between them again. And so could they.

Baby, it's Cold Outside

On our last packing day before moving out, with still a lot of packing to do, I noticed a little something moving frantically around our many red-hatted gnomes by the front sliding doors, and closer inspection revealed it to be a baby Merganser. It looked very young, was totally fluffy, and didn't look old enough to be out of the nest. It was checking out each of the gnomes red hats, and I thought it might be looking for it's red-headed mother.

I went outside and picked it up. It tried to get away from me at first, but as soon as it felt how warm my hands were, it pressed against me and hunkered down and got quiet. I was holding it cupped in my hands, it was so tiny it disappeared inside the ball my fingers made. I held it between my breasts to get it warmer, and could feel it's little life, totally dependent on me now, warming up. It had been really cold. Every time I opened my hands a little bit, it peeped and looked up at me, and I thought, "Oh, damn, I can't let this little guy go. It's too late out to find it's mother, it's too cute, it's too cold, I want to hug it, I want to keep it."

I carried the baby around while I tried to find it's family. I walked up and down the river's edge, holding the baby out so it could be seen by birds flying overhead, but no merganser parents flew over or swam by, and it was getting darker. Back inside, I tried to find some information on what to do, but with everything packed, I decided to call my wonderful neighbor on the ridge who had aviaries and ask his advice. He was kind enough to come by and take the duckling off my hands, literally. He told me later he kept it overnight in his house, then took it to work, where a wildlife rehabilitation expert from the county took it in. As I recall, they decided to keep it at the wildlife center because it had imprinted on people, so it became an education ambassador of sorts at the center. Maybe I should have left it alone to become fox food, but I just couldn't do that. Since then I've really wanted to raise a duckling, but no longer live in an area where that is possible. I play Mother Nature to a much smaller population of birds these days.

American Dipper

We saw a variety of wading birds along the river. Almost every time we were looking we could find an American Dipper. Fascinating birds that swim underwater, upstream to find food, but are not ducks. They also stand in one place for a while to see what flows past, and while they do that, they make little dipping motions with their whole body, hence the name. They are shaped like a slightly smaller short-tailed American robin, and they can swim underwater because they have a special oil gland they use to groom with that makes them waterproof, so to speak. They move around under water almost as fast as a baby Merganser. But they are a nondescript dark gray, and they blend in with the rocks in the river. I've noticed they are not too afraid of hawks, I wonder if the dipping makes them look, from overhead, like rocks with water flowing over them. That's what they look like to me, when looking down from the bridge. They can be hard to find even when you know what you're looking for, much like the green heron.

Green Heron

This heron is like a baby brother to the blue heron. It's smaller, about 14 inches from beak to tail, and has shorter, bright orange legs. It's got a crest on the top of it's head, but that isn't usually visible. It's neck and shoulders are reddish brown and it has a smaller version of the extend-able neck that herons are known for. We never saw this bird in the middle of the river, only on the very edges of the water where it's less than a foot deep. They are hard to find when you're looking for them, but almost any time we spent a couple of hours sitting on the bank watching the wildlife, we saw a green heron. They walk ever so slowly along, and sometimes you get to see them catch a fish with a quick strike.

Blue Heron

Blue herons are large, graceful birds. They have a wing span of nine feet, and a long, extend-able neck. They have a white head with a black crest off the back and grayish blue bodies. We would see them perching on the bridge railing, looking down into the water in a place where, for a few years, we saw a lot of crawdads, although I never saw a great heron catch a crawdad. We saw them wading through the river, too. They are experts at slow-motion walking, to keep from scaring the fish, but when they catch a fish, their head moves lightening quick as they extend their necks, and they catch fish about three to five inches long.

It was beautiful to see them take off flying from the railing of the bridge. One jump up and they were opening those giant wings and slowly flapping, using the air currents from their downward dive to lift them. They don't need many flaps to be on their graceful way when they take off from a high perch. Unfortunately, we only saw them singly, and never saw them roost or nest.

Orb Weaving Spiders

Just outside our front door, all through the warmer months, a swarm of hover flies would form a competition for airspace. We would have to wave our arms as we passed to keep from hitting them. So we were thrilled when an orb weaver spider took up residence there. We sort of trained it to make it's webs above our heads so we could walk under them, by moving some of it's guy wires and attaching them higher, and eventually, it stopped putting it's web in our way.

We had orb weavers at the door for about five years and they took care of the hover flies and moths for us. I would clean up the area with a Webster duster every few weeks, clearing out the old webs, and it would immediately make a new one. I thought the flies came because of the stillness in the air made by the "L" shaped building, but I never had that verified by an expert.

The orb weavers also loved to make webs on the wire fencing on the bridge. The crap that got stuck to those webs was informative. It was all debris floating through the air, stuff that could easily go up our noses, stuff we didn't want up our noses. It was surprising to find the air was not actually clean in the woods, even though we felt it was cleaner than city streets. The difference is that the dirt in the air in the woods is not black dirt, like city air-dirt is. Spiders on the bridge had to remake their webs more often than did the spider at the front door because of the air currents each dealt with, covering the webs on the bridge with so much dust and dirt, bugs won't stick.

Hummingbirds Love the Redwoods

There is only one hummingbird species that is a year round resident of the west coast, the Anna's Hummingbird. I had been feeding many of these birds in Mountain View, but since I wanted to see who came by naturally without my putting food out, I hadn't seen any hummingbirds in Big Sur at all. But my year of observing was up, and I had bought a package of suet bird food, and I was holding this package in my hand while I was standing outside, talking to Rick about where to hang it.

I noticed a hummingbird following the package around as it sailed through the air and went every which way, because I was talking with my hands. Turns out there was a picture of red and purple flowers on the front of the suet package, and the bird was trying hard to feed from them. So instead of hanging the suet up, I hung up two hummingbird feeders. I hung one by the front sliding doors and the other so we could see it from our bedroom. They each had a defender immediately. Hummers only need to defend if there is an interloper, and there were many interlopers, oh, so many. After not seeing a single hummingbird the entire year, we couldn't believe how many hummingbirds were zipping around.

So many birds were fighting over the feeders, I put up another feeder, then another, then another, until I had 10 feeders up, evenly distributed across our two acres. It was like hummingbird city, so many birds zooming by, so close to us, so much whirring of wings. We came to believe the sound of the light-sabers in the Star Wars movie was made from recording hummingbirds.

Activity at the feeders right outside our house were the only ones we could watch closely, though, and the activity was intense. I'm not exactly sure why there was so much more defending of the feeder by the front door, especially since it seemed that the bird defending that feeder was also defending two other feeders. Maybe the time he spent chasing interlopers from the feeders farther away, gave other birds time to sneak in. He could see all three feeders from his chosen perch just 10 feet above the house, which was a thin, bare, mostly dead frond of Redwood. But these contests were so vicious, we thought these birds might be stabbing each other in the chest with their long, thin bills, their built-in swords.

Anna's Tiny Body

We did find the body of an Anna's hummingbird just 10 feet from the feeder at the front door. This was a really fascinating find. At first I thought the bird might be alive and just entangled in the duff, and I was on a rescue mission to set it free. But no, it was quite dead. Its face and body feathers were mostly all intact and they are sooo tiny, but its eyes were white, and most of the front of its chest was gone, which lead us to believe it really had been stabbed to death by a competitor. All its organs were gone, and the only thing that remained of the insides was what looked like the back and sides of the ribcage.

Other than chicken and turkey, I had never really seen a birds ribcage and this seemed different. The bones themselves looked like they were made from upholstery thread, and rather than the standard ribcage we have, where the ribs are separate bones, almost like fingers holding our organs, these bones looked more like woven lattice for the birds back. The front of the chest, including the bones, was missing, so we couldn't see how they might have worked or joined together. But the bones that were left looked more like an actual cage than what we have in our chests. And the bones were brown, not white, because they were not totally dried out yet, I guess. I don't know how long this bird had been dead, but I suspect for only a day or so, as I was filling the feeders every day and would have seen it. When I search on-line to see the skeletons of hummingbirds, they are all white, so maybe they are bleached for presentation. Maybe what we saw as lattice was part of the muscle or tendons that allow the chest to expand. I don't know, but I hope I don't find out by seeing another dead hummingbird.

There are a lot of flowers in the mountain ridges along the coast of California, and hummingbirds use the nectar from them to survive their trips up and down the coast as they migrate for better weather and nesting sites. We saw the Anna's year round, but in the spring and fall we would also see the rufus and Alan's. So we had orange, magenta and golden sparkling gems flying by our windows and zipping through the trees. And if we went outside wearing clothes with flowers on them, the birds would fly right up and check us out.

These are smart birds and they know who fills the feeders. They don't trust anybody, really, but I could sit on the deck with a hummingbird feeder in my hand and they would eventually come down and check me out, flying back and forth around my face, and finally settling down to feed. But I never got the sense that I was trusted the way the turkeys trusted me.

Birds Fight with Swords

Birds stabbing each other was a new one on me, even though I'm an experienced bird watcher. One year we had two pairs of robins fighting over nesting territory in our yard. We had seen them flying around each other, screaming, and diving at each other in the trees around the house, and one morning I looked out to see the two female robins fighting on the ground, with their mates watching from different perches in the trees, about 20 feet above the females, and about 20 feet apart from each other. One female was face-down on the ground, and the other was standing on her back, stabbing her between her wings, over and over, with her beak, while the other birds screamed.

Our beloved American robin, that beautiful, stoic symbol of our peaceful, yet self-sufficient selves, was duking it out with another robin. I ran out the door straight for them, screaming and waving my arms around. We just don't allow that kind of behavior here at our house, thank you very much. All the Robins flew away, much to my surprise, so I don't know how damaged the bottom bird was. We saw only one pair of robins raising a family there that year, and never did find a dead Robin's body anywhere, but a body like that would be a great find for another animal, so it probably wouldn't have lasted long.

Puff and Bluff

Most birds use "puff and bluff" to intimidate other birds, and they don't usually have to have to resort to physical fights. The hummingbird's wars and the fighting robins were some of the worst things we saw, other than turkey fights and standard, hawk predator behavior. We saw some of that. A bit more than I preferred. The cruelty of an animal chasing, catching and then eating alive another animal, without killing it first, is hard for me to balance with the beauty of nature. I don't think I need to see things like that to be able to recognize the beauty of flowers and good friendships, and the power of evil, but maybe it does take an understanding of the whole range of good to evil to be able to pick a spot on the scale for ourselves to aspire to.

Red Shouldered Hawks Stalk

We saw more red-shouldered hawks than any other hawks, magnificent, beautiful flying machines that move silently through the woods searching for other birds to eat. They are a bit different from other hawks because they've given up some wing span in exchange for having deeper wings, a trade that gives them maneuverability to fly quietly through close quarters in the forest. We saw them make sharp, swift turns trying to catch juncos.

I guess if I needed to eat birds to survive, I would choose juncos, too. They're usually in a large flock, and they're just enough bigger than chickadees to be slow enough to catch, for a hawk of that size. We saw them stalking juncos a lot. But I think they really wanted to eat the biggest prize in the woods, the endangered band-tailed pigeon. We never saw a hawk take a pigeon, thankfully, but we saw them try, and we saw pigeon feathers and body parts strewn about on the ground often just after we'd seen the hawks, so it's pretty easy to assume the hawks ate the pigeons. But it could have been Bob-cat, fox, coyote, domestic dog or cat, or even feral cat.

Hawk Hunting Style

It seemed to me the red-shouldered hawk hunted in much the same way the pygmy owl hunts. They perch quietly on a branch close to the trunk of a tree, to blend in with the trunk. Their chest and belly, and the feathers on their legs are a rich, dark rusty color in this part of CA, and they easily blend into the redwood forest. Their wings and long tail are black and white stripes, which looks like shadows and sunlight in the woods, a very good disguise. They sit silently, motionless and invisible, watching the birds feeding below, waiting for a time when something distracts their attention and they face away. Then the hawk can sail silently over the birds and catch them by surprise. They seemed most successful with this technique if the sun wasn't behind them to make a tell-tale shadow over the prey birds during attack.

Hawks are opportunists, and it doesn't always go their way. From what I've seen, it can take mature, experienced birds 3 or more attempts for every one catch. Younger, inexperienced birds can nearly die trying, if not actually die trying. But they have other strategies if they can't find food with the low energy, surprise attack way; they would resort to flying upstream and downstream, calling repeatedly in their most terrifying way to scare the birds into taking flight in fear. Then the hawks can swiftly fly by and catch the poor scared birds with those long legs and sharp talons. I don't blame the little birds for being terrified, those hawks make a call that scares me, and I'm not even being hunted. The call is startling, and it startles the birds into actions they don't want to make.

Juncos and the Sharp-Shinned Hawk

The very first day we saw this property was in late June, and there were a couple of juncos doing their sparrow-rustle-dance on some rocks at the waters edge. I had only seen juncos in Mountain View, where I lived and fed birds for years. Every time the juncos stopped by there, it was a special event because they were the only little birds with totally black heads and solid brown backs that visited us, no bars or stripes on them. And they only stayed three days. Rare equals special.

So I was thrilled when the juncos showed up en masse one day in early fall, covering so much of the ground, it looked like the ground itself was quivering because of the shuffle they do to uncover food. There were So. Many. Birds. I counted 300 in the driveway alone, using a simple bird counting formula.

With that formula you count 10 birds and estimate in your head how big a space those 10 birds take up, then count up how many areas of the same size there are with about that many birds, x 10. It's a simple way to get an estimate. But the birds were really everywhere I looked. All over the ground and shrubs, from the river level to as far up the hill as I could see. I don't think I had ever seen so many birds at one time in my life. I was in awe. The most amazing thing was I didn't have to put bird seed out to attract them. They came on their own to eat redwood seeds.

Along with black heads, they have brown backs, and from above, it's hard to know what's going on. But the sharp-shinned hawk knew.

The sharp-shinned hawk is sometimes called the sparrow hawk, because that's what it likes to eat the most, and juncos are sparrows. This hawk is about the size of a scrub jay. It also has a shortened wing span and longer tail to make tight turns quietly in the woods and the suburbs. If you have bird feeders in your yard, or your neighbor does, you've probably seen a sharp-shinned hawk. They love a backyard bird feeding station! So many birds to choose from!

We saw a lot of their attempts to catch juncos, but I only saw one successful act. It was early spring and getting near the time juncos would migrate back north to have their babies in the cooler weather there. An unusually large and closely spaced flock was chowing down in the driveway. The biggest junco I have ever seen had been taking on a leadership roll that year, being the first to land in an area and announcing when they would leave for other eating grounds.

He had finished eating and perched on the top branch of the blackberry brush, overlooking the driveway, and started to sing the song they all knew meant it's time to go. While he was singing his heart out, the hawk came from behind, swooped down on that giant of a junco and caught him with his feet. It was so fast, I was in shock. We could hear the junco screaming and fortunately for me, the hawk flew him to a perch I could not see.

The flock of juncos froze, then took off in a swarm, and we didn't see them again until the next year.

Bird Activity Can Help Forecast the Weather

The first year we lived in Big Sur was a drought busting el nino event, so I didn't know that I wouldn't see that many juncos in other years. I didn't know much about the weather when we moved there, but I became a serious weather watcher, and bird activity was a part of that. In every el nino event we had, besides enormous numbers of juncos, we also had a small number of Varied Thrush visit. These birds are very much like American robins we see on lawns, but with more exotic coloring. We didn't see those birds in other years.

During el nino, the flocks of Townsend's warblers would be larger in number and would be accompanied by a larger number of ruby-crowned and golden-crowned kinglets. So these charming birds I'd never seen before became a harbinger of much rain to come; they arrived just before the start of rain. A dangerous message brought by beautiful birds. I've come to believe in life, the bad always comes paired WITH the good, always together, never far apart.

Dads Feeder Rule

During the first few years I was feeding birds and animals in Big Sur, it got out of hand quickly. So many birds and animals wanted to be fed, and I wanted to feed them. Soon I was spending way too much money and time with the animals, and my Dad came to visit to see them all. My father was an animal lover par excellence, and he was in Heaven.

We took a picture of him sitting on the deck with all the animals around him. He was there with six deer, a dozen turkeys, three squirrels, 10 band-tailed pigeons, six Steller's jays, eight acorn woodpeckers, and our dog Buddy, all sunning themselves on the deck, dust bathing, lazing around, feeding, drinking and bathing, all within a 50 foot diameter half circle of the deck. It lasted about 10 minutes before a little tussle between the turkeys and deer broke out and Buddy barked at them to settle down, which broke up the whole group. So it seems Heaven lasts about 10 minutes, tops.

But Dad gave me a tip on how to manage the feeding so I could continue to do it without causing trouble. There's always trouble, right? The first trouble we noticed was an increase in the number of ticks we found walking around on ourselves and our dog. And it seemed the deer and the turkeys liked the same plants we did, and they ate them until they were all gone. I was surprised to see a turkey nip off every flower on a plant. Flowers I wanted to look at.

Without the plants, the ground was bare and dusty, and as the turkeys and deer walked around, the dust (riverbank silt really) billowed up into the trees and waifed by the house, covering everything with layers of dust, layers and layers of dust. It started to get into the house and inside everything in the house. It was so pervasive, we've moved twice since then, and I found something the other day with Big Sur silt coating the inside. I miss the place so much, it brought tears to my eyes.

But I needed to make that dust stop, and that required having fewer birds and deer around the house. And Dad's tip was the first step, and it was so simple. He said I should limit the amount of food I put out every day. Who'da thunk it? I had been buying more and more food for them, when I should have been buying less.

At first I was horrified by the thought of not putting food out when I knew the birds were hungry. Dad convinced me when he said the birds and animals wouldn't just stop coming, or just leave totally when the food was gone, they would keep checking back throughout the day to see if I put out more food. When I learned to temper my feeding, I found out how right he was. Seasonal changes make the birds and animals change their daily habits, too, so that's the time I chose to change my feeder/feeding habits.

That fall, I stopped putting mixed bird seed, cracked corn and rolled oats on the ground in our driveway, and started putting it on the far side of our property, where there was already a wide path the animals used. We cut down some dead tanoak suckers so the animals had less spooky-space to deal with while they ate, and could feel safe bringing their children there.

I had thought animals liked dense woods, that we would find more animals there because of the density, but that wasn't totally true. The most used paths by the animals were the widest, most open paths, through the largest clearings. That way an animal can see who's coming for it with enough time to run or fly away. But they need the woods to hide and sleep.

I love the dense woods. Love the deep shade. But too dense isn't good either, not for the plants or the animals. I noticed that when the tanoaks died off and sun hit the ground in a regular pattern, the wildflowers burst out of the ground like they were going on parade. Toothwart, always the first to flower in the spring, trillium, starflower, tiger lilies, forest pansy, columbine, globe lily, Soloman's plume, and the ever present forget-me-not were suddenly prolific. I looked for these plants early on but I didn't see them regularly until about 2000, after most of the tanoak was gone.

I'm happy to hear there is an experiment going on in California and Oregon about thinning the most dense stands of wilderness to make the forest healthier and be able to withstand fires better. Let's keep the big trees big.

Universal Inter-Species Sign for All Gone

The next summer, I slowly stopped putting food out on the ground. As I was changing the feeding schedule, I discovered the Universal Inter-Species sign for all gone. The animals that knew me, knew I brought food, and they would come by and look for me. All day long. Just like people, animals and birds have a way of standing to make themselves look skinny, which makes them look hungry, and I guess I'm a sucker for that. We can see our slightly overweight dog sit up and stretch his neck to make himself look thin every night while he begs for his dinner.

But it didn't take long for them to understand my new signal, "all gone" - holding my empty hands up in the air with fingers spread, and showing them both sides of my hands were empty. Both the deer and the turkeys understood. They would look so sad. But I just had to stop the feeding. They all liked to use the same paths we did, and there was too much poop around. At some point, you have to recognize your own safety's importance.

The Damage Done

When we moved in, the forest canopy was closed, and it was moist and damp and green. But after just a couple of years feeding, the deer had eaten all the giant clover sorrel ground cover. It took years to regrow. All that dust that the turkeys scratched up looking for bugs and seeds, all landed somewhere I didn't want it. And the dust-bathing, so much dust bathing. Our path to the bridge was so dusty in the summer, it was choking us and we worried about our dogs following us, getting the dust we kicked up in their lungs, they were such short dogs. We let them go ahead of us, instead of behind.

Just getting the deer and turkeys to use the farthest path from our front door made a huge difference. And the real key to that turned out to be letting our new little dogs chase them. Our two little, size-blind, chihuahua/terrier mix dogs were pretty sure they could take on any and all comers. I would give the deer and turkey the all gone signal, and if they didn't believe me and move along, Vito and LambChop got to chase them. And there was always some deer poo for the dogs to chow down on. So it was doubly worth it to them.

The other way we found to get a flock of turkeys to leave the area is by sticking a lambswool duster outside the door. We took to calling it a *cat on a stick*. As long as the turkeys didn't see us holding the stick, it worked. It worked like magic, too. Just putting the fuzzy wool part outside the door, without the stick being seen by the birds would cause the whole flock to go running and flying away at once. It was comical. We discovered this when Rick stuck the duster out the front door to shake it, and they all took off before he got himself outside to do the shaking. The duster was the same color as a mountain lion and maybe that's what scared them. We found this worked for some deer, not all, but it worked for all turkeys.

Don't worry about the deer or the turkeys. Their path was not foiled, they were always able to reach the spot they wanted to go, a shady place where they liked to nap in the afternoons in the summer. They just took the far path, and our plants started to recover. In winter, the deer were mostly on the tops of the ridges, where it was sunnier and warmer. I think the Indigenous people, the early settlers and many other animals and birds do the same thing.

Metal Dog Crate to Feed Birds

I still liked feeding birds, so I decided to try feeding just the little birds. But I had to find a way to keep bigger birds out. I wanted to feed chickadees, sparrows, and juncos. I had an extra-large dog crate made of black metal wire and the wires on the cage were in inch apart. I thought the chickadees could manage that, since they use nest boxes with a hole that big.

I hung some tube feeders inside with black oil sunflower seeds and millet, and put the cage up against a fallen redwood log that was big enough to totally hide the cage from the other side, to make the birds feel safe. I put a couple inches of dirt on the floor of the cage, so the sparrows could do their shuffle with out breaking their tiny little toes on the cage wires, and sprinkled some seed on that. And I put a birdbath on the ground nearby.

I hoped, since the little birds were already coming to that bath, they would see the tube feeders in the cage. They loved it. They got so good at getting inside the cage, it looked like it was open-sided.

Both the chickadees and the juncos were able to swoop down from a perch 50 to 100 feet up, fly right through the cage bars, and land on the tube feeder perches. I never saw one miss or hit the wire bars of the cage. This was advanced flying, practiced tactical maneuvers that were such fun to watch. These acrobatic birds are proud of themselves, you can hear them congratulate themselves with a little cheer when they land, like a fist pump.

They're having fun, challenging each other to perches, and commenting on each others performance. Chickadees have something to say about everything. And they don't seem to fear any other birds. They will fly in to land on a perch a woodpecker is on, they are so brave. But they are so cute, even the other birds think they're cute and let them get away with so much, stealing of perches and turns in line for food. In all the years there, though, I never saw a chickadee touch the ground. Just didn't happen, not even to get seed on the floor inside the cage. I don't know why. I've seen them get pieces of peanut they've dropped to the ground in other locals, but not in Big Sur. Just not done.

Doves by the Numbers

The band tailed pigeon is the largest dove in North America, at 13 1/2 inches from beak to tail. (Generally speaking, the terms pigeon and dove are interchangeable, although I refer to the entire group as doves). The band tailed is endangered because it's a forest bird looking for acorns, and both forest and acorns are in dwindling supply, in California, anyway. The doves were thrilled with the platform feeder I put up. I wanted to feed acorn woodpeckers, though, another bird struggling due to acorn loss. Woodpeckers are more fun to watch, with their red heads and threatening beaks. Watching them eye up another bird to convince it to leave is fun. They barely have to move to convince a junco to get lost. Doves are different, when I put up the platform feeder, I hadn't realized the specific strategy doves use to get food.

Doves swamp the area with so many of themselves, no other species can get in, and they are such big birds they can get away with it. No matter how many birds were on the platform, they could converge and take it over. Then, they would have a rather orderly display of taking turns at the food. With so many on the platform, when one lands, one has to fall off, so they eat as much as they can, as fast as they can. They are starving and empty the feeder so fast. But much as I would like to single-handedly revive the species by providing food, I just don't have enough food to give them. They are expensive birds to feed. I eventually took the platform down and put up peanut butter feeders. The pigeons don't really like that. But they perched above our house forever after that, pooping purple from eating wild blackberries, and continued to watch for whatever food I put out.

So much so that one day I noticed a ruckus inside the wire cage and saw it was a pigeon stuck inside and freaking out, banging itself on the sides of the cage, trying to escape. I knew if I went outside, directly to the cage, the bird would probably damage itself trying to get away from me. I decided to walk backwards to the cage, slowly, to see if that calmed it down. I didn't want it to see my eyes or teeth, or it would think I wanted to eat it.

Now, this bird knows me, it has seen me putting food out, so it knows there might be a benefit to having me nearby, maybe I'm bringing food. And the bird did calm down and stop thrashing about. It just sat on the ground, I could see that from the reflection in our sliding glass doors. So I backed up to the cage and opened the door behind my back, and the dove took off. I was happy to see it fly, and not limp out. After that experience, I turned the cage upside down and wired closed the tray slot the dove got inside through, and that never happened again.

Birds Bring Star-Flowers

I changed the location of that cage multiple times so I could refresh the dirt on the bottom, and every place I put it got a real shot of bird-poop fertilizer mixed with two inches of forest potting soil mulch, which really encouraged native plants to grow profusely. We had so many star-flowers grow in these places, it was like a solid ground cover. You would think I had dropped star-flower seed in these places, but I don't think star-flower seed is actually available to buy, it's just a tiny, delicate native plant, that grows a whirl of deep green leaves with a small, pink, star shaped flower on a very thin stem, above the greenery. And the most fascinating thing about it is that the flower grows another point every year, so you can tell how old the flower bulb is by how many points are on the star. Delightful! I wish I could buy this plant, but I've never seen it available for sale.

Mountain Lion Avoidance

One of the first things you learn in the woods in California is how to avoid Mountain Lions. They might kill you, or worse, just maim you. You should learn how to avoid them if you're in California. It's not a joke, and don't depend on what I say, I'm not an expert. But we did a few things to protect ourselves. We carried hunting knives on our belts. We kept them sharp. We wore extra large coats so we could make ourselves look larger just by holding our arms out, preferably with a knife in hand.

My feeling is a big cat knows how sharp it's own claws are, it can recognize other sharp things in our hands. We kept our dogs close as we walked at night and rattled our keys as we walked. We used large, heavy MagLites when we were out at night letting the dogs out to pee or coming home after dark. We never encountered a Mountain Lion outside, that we were aware of anyway.

I saw only one mountain lion during our time there, early one morning, on the other side of the river, walking downstream on the bank. I was cozy inside, thrilled and scared at the same time. This was a real life "land shark." I looked over my shoulder a lot more after that. There is only one tan/golden/tawny animal with an exceptionally long tail that has a dark tip. I watched till it was out of sight.

Over the years we heard tell of mountain lions that used our driveway as a regular thoroughfare. A mountain lion walking down our driveway slowly would get a chance to see a lot of ground, on both sides of the river and pretty far up and down the river without being exposed itself. There were big rocks the cat could hide in while watching for the deer to take their nap on the shady island. Much as I worried about encountering a big cat, especially while getting water to run, I'm happy to say I never knew of my life being in danger.

Coyote Sighting

We had only one experience with coyote, although we thought they were probably around because we could hear them sometimes. That one interaction was with a small coyote that was heading from the river up the hill. I saw it from the house and followed quietly on the fire road. I wanted to see where it went, but I made a noise that scared it, and it ran off the path and up the hill, and from what I could tell, it stopped and hid in a dark patch of I don't know what, about 25 feet up. I went back to the house and got Rick and the BB gun, and pointed out to Rick the dark patch I thought the coyote was in. Rick had much better aim at the time than I did, and shot a BB that hit the dark patch dead center.

The coyote jumped up and ran up the hill so fast, we laughed out loud. We really didn't expect that. I thought for sure the coyote would have left when I left to get Rick. Brian had just given us the BB gun and we were looking for an excuse to use it, which is why he tried the shot, but I'm pretty sure we didn't hurt the coyote, because it sounded like it hit leaves, not fur covered skin.

The BB gun was a real pump-action Daisy just like in the movie "The Christmas Story," and from my research, it seems it can only hurt the eyes of young, human children. I got pretty good with it, though, and no young children were harmed. If the deer refused to stop eating the few roses I was able to grow, I shot them on the hip with the BB gun. I could see the BB bounce off the deer, so I was merely an annoyance, the power of the Daisy is not killer, just fun.

Salamanders

There are a lot of salamanders on the bank of a shaded river. Within days of moving in, we were sitting on a bench at the edge of the cliff in our back yard, watching the river go by, when we noticed an orange-ish, 3-inch long, wet-looking salamander just three feet in front of us, running at what looked like top speed for a salamander. It was surprisingly fast. It ran across the path and dove into a tiny hole in the ground on the other side. We didn't see anything chasing it so we didn't know why it was in such a hurry. But I had just been thinking about what or who made that hole, and contemplating whether to dig into it to find out. So the salamander answered the question of what that hole was for, and I was glad I hadn't ruined it by digging it out to learn for myself.

We saw three kinds of salamander there. We saw two of them a lot. The orange-ish one, which I've never been able to identify for certain, and the salamander that looks like a dark brown, very skinny, 5-inch long snake, with teeny-tiny, barely visible legs. I think that one is the

California slender salamander. We saw both those kinds whenever we lifted a rock or log or planter or paver. Salamanders breath through their skin, so they need to be in shady, moist places, under leaf litter or solid things. Whenever we moved things around outside, we had to collect the salamanders we uncovered and move them to a safer, darker place. Every time. It was fun to find them because they were hard to see even when exposed. It was like a real-life "Highlights" magazine.

A few times we saw an arboreal salamander, a salamander who lives in trees. It was ghostly white and looks almost transparent, about five inches long. We saw it in a crack in the bark of "Old Tom" the old redwood. We were able to see it a few times at night with our flashlights, but we didn't have good enough camera phones at that time to get a picture. We didn't get a really good look because we didn't want to disturb it by shining a bright light on it for that long. I don't want some stranger taking a brightly lit picture of me in my house, I'm pretty sure the salamanders feel the same way.

Bats

We moved to Big Sur in the fall, and one of the first things we noticed in the early evening was the bats. There were so many, they seemed to pour through the sky, down the fire road, past our house and down the driveway to the river, where they dispersed up and down stream. The wildlife taking advantage of man made structures. They were using our fire road and driveway as their own highway to the river, but at 50 to 100 feet off the ground

There were two kinds of bat, as far as we could tell, a larger bat, about the size of a Scrub Jay, and a smaller bat, about the size of a junco. I was never able to identify them with confidence, they don't perch anywhere, so I couldn't see them with binoculars, but between the two of them, they were able to eat from the tiniest biting fly to large moths. Mammals that fly. That bats aren't birds is hard to fathom. And where do they sleep? I didn't know of any caves around there, but the bats were here so I had some research to do.

After the parade of bats passed on their way to the river we could see some of them flying about in between the house and cabin, and if we walked along the bank of the river near the water's edge, we would see a lot more. One evening I was inside watching, standing about about six inches behind the sliding glass door and I saw a small bat flitting around about 20 feet away.

Very quickly a giant mosquito like bug flew by the window at my eye level, about six inches from the window, and the bat was there instantly. The bat flew straight up to the window, mouth open so big it's head seemed to disappear behind it, and it was so close to me, I could see the blood vessels in the back of it's throat. It snapped it's mouth shut and the bug was so big, it's wings and legs stuck out of the bat's mouth as it took off. It was such an intimate encounter. The bat was able to maneuver so precisely that it didn't get much closer to the window than the bug had been, and turned sharply as it made it's get away.

But we weren't able to see the bats return in a parade, apparently they return, each at their own pace. But we never saw them flying about in the morning, not even as the sun came up.

We learned that bats sleep in the deep, dark crevices of redwood tree bark. There is a lot of that kind of bark in the older forest, where trees are more than 200 years old. The trees in front of our house were older than that, so they had plenty of bedrooms for the bats. We know they used them, we found out in a disturbing way.

We heard a ruckus coming from so high up in the trees, we couldn't see the actual birds making the noise. But we knew from the sounds that Crows were involved. A murder of crows? A murder for sure, but not of a crow. We could hear shrieking and screaming that didn't sound at all like crows, getting closer and closer. Looking up we saw a bat floating down, face up, wings fully extended, screaming over and over. It landed flat on its back, wings out and it continued screaming.

We could hear the crows ruckus as they hopped down the tree branches like stairs, could see them watching the bat and "caw"ing to each other, I don't know how many crows, maybe three, but they made so much noise, it sounded like five.

When the bat landed we could see a huge wound in the bat's chest, a wound it could not recover from, even if it had landed in a wildlife surgical center. The wound looked big enough to match the size of a crow beak. But there was nothing we could do to help the bat. We left the house out the back way for a walk on the river bank, where the sound of the water rushing on it's way to the ocean was loud enough to keep us from hearing that screaming. When Mother Nature is so harsh, all we can do to feel better is find some other place where Mother Nature seems kind, and let the beauty of that wash over us. That was the bad, now lets focus on the good.

When we returned, there was no evidence of any ruckus, no bat, no crows, just the rustling of the redwoods in the breeze, with the dappled sunlight making even the air seem soft and comforting.

Part 4: Transformations

El Nino 1998

The real test of my winter supply program came in the spring of 1998, when an el nino storm washed away so much of the road between Carmel and our house. We were stuck there for months. But we were okay. Local government told everyone right away that only folks who were able to be self-sufficient could stay in town, everyone else would have to leave. And within a few days, we were isolated with all the other folks who were self-sufficient. There were no transients, no strangers walking down the highway, no tourists, we knew everyone we saw in town lived there, or was there to help.

The isolation provided a real sense of security, and ease. There were CHP officers guarding the entrances to our town, making sure only residents were allowed through. We didn't have to be on our guard so much, everyone we met was in the same boat we were in, counting supplies and wondering how long we could last. And the feeling of ease that came with all that surprised me. This is the feeling we expected to find when we moved to the country. The feeling we thought we'd have living rurally, all the time. But it really only comes in short bursts of superficiality. Security is so fleeting.

Finally, notices were posted on the few store fronts in Big Sur, telling of a way made for locals to form a caravan to get to town for supplies. Some neighbors were obviously surprised to see us in the caravan, surprised we could be self sufficient, and that was satisfying; we were such idiots when we moved in. We wondered how many locals lost bets on how long we'd be able to hack it in Big Sur.

We all had to be in line, in our car, with everyone else when they started the caravan. We had to be back in line to get the caravan home by about 3pm, when they opened the road for the caravan to return. The condition of the road was just mind-blowing. It made me much less likely to go anywhere in a big rain, ever again.

We could see how the disaster happened as we drove by: basins on the east side of the highway that had always collected rain and shuttled it under the highway, through culverts, to the ocean side, broke. The culverts were not large enough to feed the excess rain through. The basins backed up with water so high, the pressure pushed the culverts and the roadway right into the ocean. Not just one culvert, almost all of them.

Where the culverts had been, so much dirt washed away, the ground level was lowered in each spot by about 25 feet. Where the road surface was still intact, the road was at a higher elevation. So the caravan cars went up and down a lot of hills on that drive, where the road had been gradual inclines before. And the lower elevations were all just dirt that had been graded for us to drive on. We could see how loose the surface was from how much dirt flew from the wheels of the car in front of us.

Over time, workers put in gigantic culverts, and filled the dirt back in, so the finished road surface was back up to the elevation it had always been. But that day, it was a long, slow ride, with a CHP escort, so no speeding was seen. We finally got to town and had about five hours to get our supplies.

We were in Costco when we realized we could tell who lived in Big Sur by how big a bag of rice they had in their cart. I guess we were all rushing around, too, trying to get everything we needed and get back in line for the caravan, or miss our only chance to get home for another month or two. I don't remember exactly how many caravans they made available for supplies, but we didn't go every time because we didn't always need more supplies.

Since the road north to Carmel was not accessible without a caravan for months, there was a time when we needed to get prescriptions filled, and the only way out was Highway One south, then over Nacimiento/Ferguson Rd., to King City, where there is another Costco. We had to transfer our prescriptions to the new store the day before the trip. We had never taken this route, and the directions were hand written and sketchy. There were no map apps to use, no smart phones to help us find our way, we had no Garmin. But Rick got us there, and back, and I'm so glad he was driving, he has an excellent sense of direction, and always got us where we needed to go. It's a long trip, over three hours from our house when the road is in good condition, and it, too had been damaged by the rains. Speed limits there were only 25 mph, so even slower still.

But by far, the scariest part for me was when we were driving south on Highway one, through Lucia, where the road had also washed out. The first time I saw Lucia was in February 1975, on my first vacation trip to California. When I looked out over the back deck of the lodge there (we were the only folks there at the time!) I fell in love with California. I had been living in Pennsylvania, and absolutely had to move to CA. I had fallen in love with the coast, the blue, blue ocean, and the dramatic green mountains that came right up to the blue. And right there on that back deck, I knew I'd be back to California. So Lucia made quite an impression on me.

Now I could see the restaurant in the distance as we approached, but my memory of it is surrounded with dirt, not beautiful green mountains. This restaurant is 500 feet above the ocean. The clearest memory I have of that day is driving from road surface onto dirt, following a car that was following the CalTrans bulldozer that was grading the one lane surface flat for us to drive on. It was one lane carved into the side of a cliff.

The ground was much softer than I was comfortable with and there was no shoulder, no guardrail. When I looked out the window, I could see about six inches of dirt road past our tires, and then straight down to the ocean. I'm both shocked and grateful they let us drive over it. I quickly averted my gaze, as if the extra weight of my head tilting to look down might send us hurtling over the edge. I leaned to the left till we got to blacktop again. Rick said this was the hardest part of the drive for him, too, because he really couldn't tell just how close he was to that edge. I don't know what would have happened if we weren't in our trusty Subaru Forester. We never got stuck in that car.

So Rick did the driving out and heavy lifting for me that day, and drove home, too. By the time we passed the Lucia Lodge on our way home again, a larger shoulder was available. Remembering the look down to the ocean that day still makes my heart rise in my chest. I'm really glad we didn't hit a soft spot and get stuck there, or slide off the edge of the cliff.

Hats off to the CalTrans driver, just doing his job. These guys risk their lives to make the world safer for others. Yes, they get paid, but man, these guys work hard and get the job done. Unless you have a helicopter, you have to use the roads to get to Big Sur, just like everyone else. And, WOW, it is beautiful! Thank you CalTrans workers!

The Bridge

The reason we had to keep so much winter supply on hand, more than most folks in Big Sur, was because of the footbridge. We knew it had been torn down by water in the 80's, so any reasonable person would know it could happen again. If a storm took our bridge out, we wanted to be able to survive on our side for as long as possible, because there was no way to know for sure how long a time we might wait for rescue. As we watched giant tree trunks with large branches roaring downstream, we thought our bridge could easily be taken out. Especially because it was so old and rickety.

When we had the chance to improve it, we did. We had talked early on about replacing the bridge completely, but the stock market gods did not favor us, so we did the only thing we could, hired local and worked without permits. We started to make repairs at one end of the bridge. We thought we'd repair a few things, maybe get new "down" wires. We didn't yet realize that everything we tried to fix was connected to something else that also needed to be fixed just to make the connection.

We started with the most obvious thing we could see. The structure on the house side of the bridge, that held the bridge wires up, was failing. There was a wooden structure, but instead of a column on the downstream side, the wires were attached to a tanoak, and by 1998, we knew that tree wouldn't last long because of Sudden Oak Death.

One day, while carrying a cast iron bird feeder hook to it's spot, I passed the tree and noticed a small hole in the bark. I pushed the end of the hook into that hole and it went through nearly the entire trunk. After a little digging there it was clear the tree was not actually providing structural support to the bridge, there was only a three inch diameter section of wood holding up the top of the tree. It was a lesson in how strong wood is though, because the top was huge.

The other side of this tree-made-support was a laurel tree, also not in great shape. And there was a bend in the bridge wires at the structure, made so the redwood could be the support weight, even though it was not in a straight line from the other side of the bridge. We hired a local crew who got started by making plans to build a concrete pillar to replace the tanoak. Before they began work on the pillar, they investigated how to move the wires over to it, when they realized the wires were too old and brittle to be able to be moved. They were 50 year old, 5-strand wire; todays wire rope is made of multiple strands in each of the five wires, making it a lot stronger. So, yet another thing to work out.

We thought, while we're making repairs, maybe we could get the wires off the 1000 year old redwood, so it didn't have to hold up the bridge anymore. So we needed to make a deadman on the house side of the bridge. We found a spot that was perfect. It was in a straight line from the other side of the bridge, and apparently, something had been there before, because we could see a depression in the soil that was an obvious square, and just the right size for us. Some things are meant to be.

As the guys dug it out, they found it was easy to dig, just sand, no rocks. About five and a half feet down, they found an old, clay, septic pipe. We thought that was good, we didn't disturb anything new. They had their books out and got all the measurements they needed to make the re-bar cage that went inside the hole, and they poured the concrete on Christmas Eve. That's hard work, we were pretty astounded by their diligence, coming from the tech world where almost no one works Christmas Eve, or the last half of December, really. We gave them extra for their trouble.

But there was one guy who worked for us so long, he was more like our best friend. Brian was the nicest guy, excellent trombone player, and all around big guy who could do big jobs. Brian did them all, and well. We'd have been lost without him. He did 90% of the bridge work himself, and so many other things besides. He could make anything fun, so he made everything fun. When we look back at our time there, we think the best times, the most fun we had, was our morning meetings with Brian. Working out the specifics of the bridge design with him was fabulously fun. We talked and laughed about the news and events of the day, too. And he was so good at making things happen, he made the bridge happen.

We talked a lot about how to make it possible to lift the bridge floor up higher in a storm, to get it out of the way of branches that might get caught up, and tear it down. We added giant turnbuckles to the wires on the house side that could lift the floor two feet, once you disconnected the suspended part of the bridge from the decks at each end. We're proud of that design. We know it works, too, because Blaze Engineering raised the floor once to make a repair for us.

Brian organized a crew whenever he needed additional help, he found equipment, found suppliers, did research, learned how to do things he hadn't done before, and did them for us. He brought all the wood, wire and tools to the bridge project, and I got the connectors from Orchard Supply Hardware. There were many, many trips to town to get all the parts together.

We started the project with a local Big Sur Contractor, Richard Trotter, and he brought Brian with him and introduced him to us. It was Brian and Richard who discovered the bridge wires were not connected to a deadman on one end. By this time, we had found so many, many things wrong with every thing on the property, we were both not surprised, and shocked. Even if we had new wires to attach to those augers, we felt the need for a concrete block of weight to hold the bridge up.

Trouble was, the augers were sunk into a hill that was not on our property, not even on an easement. And the wires were so low across the driveway, a fire truck couldn't get under them to come and put out a fire. We worried about that a lot, we had to do something. We thought the only possible place to put the deadman was under the driving surface of the driveway, and Richard agreed. It was already a driveway, there shouldn't be an environmental problem there.

Years later, after the bridge was completely repaired, we hired a local man, Terry, to dig holes with his CAT and install posts. We needed the posts to keep vehicles from driving over the cliff where the old bridge's landing had been. But he couldn't get his auger to dig the last hole, and it was because there was no dirt where we wanted to put the post. It was solid concrete. It was the original deadman that the wires had been ripped from in 1983. We had dug the hole for the new deadman about six inches away from the original, and never knew it till then.

Richard Trotter had supervised the making of both deadmen, and we felt good about that, he had so much experience with projects like ours. Unfortunately for us, Richard took on another project after that, but Brian was able to complete the job for us mostly on his own over the course of a couple of years. We could just barely afford him, and almost every year, the tech start-up Rick worked for would implode just before Christmas and reformulate itself into something else a few months later, and we had to lay Brian off during that time as well. Very frustrating.

Part of our bridge design was to ensure that in a time of very high water, we could disengage the bridge wires without it tearing the connections out of the deadman. That way we could reconnect to the deadman later. In case of a flood, we had a multi-part plan. First, we would raise the suspended section by crossing the bridge and disconnecting the suspended part from the decking on that end. Then come back and disconnect on our end. Then we could turn the turn-buckles enough to raise the suspended section two feet.

If the river rose higher, we hoped to call Blaze Engineering to come over and disconnect the bridge wires from the deadman on that side of the river, and let the bridge go, so we could reclaim the bridge from the slower moving side, as had been done in 1983, and still have a working deadman to re-connect with, and hopefully still have suspension towers on each end to re-hang the wires from. That was the plan. A plan we hoped we would never need to carry out. We never did.

Using wire rope was new to us and Brian. We all read up on it. We had to calculate the weight of all the parts of the bridge that would be hanging off the suspension wires, which, as I recall was 7000 lbs. We chose suspension wires that could support 22,000 lbs. That way we could have heavy things moved across the bridge, like, say, another pellet stove!

We learned that wire rope stretches when first in place. That meant we could get the whole thing built, and soon after, the bridge would sag and have to be tightened up. As it sagged, all the "down" wires that connect the floor boards to the big suspension wires above, would become misaligned, and have too much tension in some spots and not enough in others. The connections would have to be realigned on the big wires above, requiring a ladder on the bridge. There were 42 pairs of down wires on the bridge and all 84 connectors would have to be repositioned multiple times as the wires stretched with use.

That was unacceptable. Rick and Brian and I talked about this a lot and decided to hang the new suspension wires above the old wires and hang weights on them to stretch them out before anything else was connected. We just happened to have a bunch of antique, yellow bricks that had been used to make a yellow brick path to our door, and they were used as the weights. Brian made 84 bundles of bricks. He taped the bricks together on 2x4's with heavy duty tape. He hung them on the big wires, from the connectors the new down wires would soon be hung.

Brian did all that work before he built the landing at the end of the bridge on the highway side. Building that landing took enough time, the wires were stretched as much as they needed to be, and we never had to reposition the placement of the down wires on the big wires.

But now, it was time for the real magic to happen, replacing one suspended section of the bridge at a time, from one side to the other. We were able to use the bridge almost the entire time the work was in progress, and sometimes it was scary. The new section was higher than the old sections, sometimes by two feet, and we had to step up or down, depending on which direction we were going. The two levels were not connected, and were independently bouncy, and there was no railing to grab. It was hard for me sometimes, but the little dogs had no troubles with this at all. There were just a few days we had to walk across the river, stepping on stones, to get to our car.

The old bridge had wire fencing from the railings to the floorboards, so we couldn't fall out and neither could our dogs, but this had to be removed for the duration of the project. The fencing and railings were the last things to be replaced. All during this time, our little dog Vito would walk across the bridge using just the very edge of the wood, about an inch and a half wide, while he looked over the edge to the water below, the whole way. Every time. The bridge was always bouncing as we walked along, but that didn't dissuade him a bit. What was he thinking?

Brian brought a friend of his, Sean, a heavy equipment operator who was between jobs, to help with this hardest part of the job, and these two amazingly strong, great looking guys worked their butts off for us. Just as they got started, my father showed up, and tried to boss them around, and they were gracious enough to put up with him and take him out drinking after work. I'll love these guys forever for that. It took just a few weeks to get the new suspended section completely across the river, with all three of them working hard and joking constantly.

Out of earshot of my father, I told them I could make my father leave if he was getting in their way or bothering them, and they said no, they were happy to have him there. This is one of my favorite memories of Big Sur, and of my father, he was happier those few weeks than I had ever seen him. He loved working on the bridge, doing hard work, being included. Nothing is better than that. Watching these guys work, seeing the project come together, and work as planned, was one of the most satisfying experiences of our lives.

Brian was an excellent project manager, too. The three of us would talk about what needed to happen, and Brian would patiently explain why our crazy ideas wouldn't work, and he'd find a way to do it better, and make it right. He came up with great ideas about how to get things done; he was the most helpful man I've ever met. He kept track of every u-bolt, connector, cable, nut, wire, board, tool, fencing, staples, eye-hooks, small and giant turnbuckles, screws, nails, and so many other things. He found suppliers and rented machines. He put up with me, no easy task, and on top of that, he did the bulk of the actual hard work. I can't say enough good about him.

When the bridge was finished it was three feet higher, straight, flat, wide enough for a wheelchair, did not sag a bit, and bounced a lot less than the old one. The railings were at the right height, and we doubled the number of support beams and down wires holding the floor boards. It was lovely.

So lovely that every weekend, we found tourists standing in the center of the bridge, some even drinking champagne. They passed a gross amount of *private property*, and *no admission* signs to get there. Some people were stupid enough to go on the bridge even when it wasn't safe, ignoring *warning cones* and *caution signs* and *caution tape*. We found a father and his teenage son jumping up and down in the middle of the bridge, as hard and high as they could, to see how high the bridge would bounce. These people had the attitude that they were entitled to damage our property, just because it was in Big Sur, and they were visiting. It's the most obnoxious attitude I've come upon yet. That's why the folks we sold the property to decided to dismantle the bridge and remove it. We were so sorry to hear about that, but completely understood why. They owned the property on the other side of us from the river, so they didn't need the bridge. To the bouncing father and son, *you* are the reason we can't have nice things. You should be ashamed of yourselves.

I painted the bridge almost every year with paint that had granules in it so it wasn't slippery. Painting over water like that was tricky. I had to be sure not to let any paint drops fall in the river. I made myself special wire tools to use to keep drips from actually falling in the water in case I caused a drop to form. Painting the bridge was hard work, but still, a pleasure. The kingfisher would buzz me, unhappy I was on his bridge. We found the skeletons of many of his victims on the bridge, on one end, in the shade. I guess from the bridge railings, if they dropped their catch, it fell on the bridge, not in the water, as it would from a tree perch.

On clear, moonless nights, we went out to the middle of the bridge in the middle of the night with chair cushions to lie on our backs and watch the stars. We could see the Milky Way, centered in the open sky over the river, framed by ridges and trees, a clear and spectacular view of the sky. It was so dark there, the stars were brilliant. We were surprised at how much of the sky we could see from the bridge, and it was the one place we could see sunshine, when the sun was shining.

Every day we walked around our property, and toured the perimeter with our dogs, to check things out. We crossed the bridge and climbed the hill to get the mail, and on the way, if it was sunny, we would stand on the bridge with the dogs, to let the sun shine on us for 10 to 20 minutes, to get our vitamin D. The dogs loved this as much as we did. The view was great and they got to smell so many things in the open air.

It wasn't just the dogs who liked to use the bridge. We've seen turkeys in full display walk across and hop over the gate at the end, and we've seen them displaying on the railings, too. We've seen the small deer that live in Big Sur cross the bridge, and have to turn around at the gate and go back. They are the cutest deer, a separate race from the larger deer they interbreed with. And we've seen raccoons and skunk scamper across, too. The blue heron, belted kingfisher, and red-shouldered hawk all liked to perch on the bridge railings.

Crossing it any time of day or night was spectacular, no matter what the weather, and sometimes because of the weather. Crossing in a big storm with rising water so close to your feet, and so loud there is no sense in talking, raining so hard everything looks coated with gray, that can make you question your sanity. What are you doing walking over such a big, fast river, standing in the middle, watching, and listening to the rocks clang together? That's real trust in workmanship.

We loved that bridge. We knew we would never have been able to afford a place in Big Sur if it weren't for the drawbacks of that bridge and the shape it was in. Before we moved in, I had spoken by phone to the sister of the man who sold us the property. I invited her to stop by anytime, and she told me that she was using a wheelchair and wouldn't physically be able to visit, as her chair wouldn't make it across the bridge, or go over unpaved paths. That broke my heart and I decided then we had to have a bridge wide enough for wheelchairs. I tried to keep our paths covered in thick chips that had been rolled and tamped down, so a wheelchair could go across. We needed to get our wagons across, too and these changes helped us, too.

She was a delightful woman who told me the story of how she had met her husband. My recollection is that her father insisted she come to Big Sur for a holiday weekend, and she wasn't that happy about it. But she was sitting by the river when a handsome, charming man came walking along and stopped to chat with her. She said their marriage was long and very happy, and he had passed away just two years before my call. She felt the place was magical, and she assured me I would never want to leave. She was absolutely right about that.

Afterward

Much as we loved living in Big Sur and wanted to stay forever, we found it would be better for our financial future to retire elsewhere. It took two years to make that decision, to be able to face living somewhere else, and then two years to ready the property for sale. Then another two years on the market. The second year it was on the market, we were lucky to find Mike Gilson, a great real estate agent, to help us.

We knew our house had been on the market for two years when we bought it, but we had hopes that our property was so special (unusual!), it would sell quickly. Turns out it was hard for us to get into Big Sur, and much, much harder to leave.

I can't wash Big Sur out of my hair, so to speak, it will always be a big part of my being. But the densely shaded wood we bought changed so much over the time we lived there, with Sudden Oak Death and drought. And with Jali's Garage closing, the warming temps, and so much more traffic, it all made a big dent in our happiness there. We needed to go north.

About a year after leaving, we heard this quote:

"The greatest day in a man's life, after he buys his home in the country, is the day he sells it." We're still laughing about that.

Acknowledgements

Thanks go especially to my dear husband, Rick, who encouraged me to write and helped me with photos, details, formatting and all things digital.

Special thanks to my readers, Trisha Church, Connie Gutt and Kathy Kelcey. Their encouragement and comments kept me going to the finish.

Many thanks to Pam, and to Don, for inspiring me from afar.

Many thanks to Jali, Brian Moore, and Donnie Nix, for allowing me to tell these stories and use their names and photos.

Jali has retired.

*Donnie Nix, the Tree Surgeon, can be found here: www.facebook.com/DonNixTheTreeSurgeon/

*Brian Moore quit building bridges and went full time trombone. He can be found playing with The Monterey Jazz All-Stars, The Latin Jazz Collective with John Neva, The Tom Reston Band, and The Glen Miller Band. He teaches, too.

Dear Reader,

Thanks for reading my book!

If it amused you, I hope you'll consider leaving a review on Amazon.

Thanks again,

Barbara

Barbara DelMar can be reached by email at:

TurnsOut@beriwood.com